A Climate Charged

A Climate Charged

B.W. Powe

◣ MOSAIC PRESS

OAKVILLE   NEW YORK   LONDON

Canadian Cataloguing in Publication Data

Powe, B. W. (Bruce W.), 1955-
    A climate charged : essays on Canadian writing

ISBN 0-88962-259-0 (bound). - ISBN 0-88962-258-0 (pbk.).

1. Canadian literature (English) - 20th century -
History and criticism - Addresses, essays, lectures.*
I. Title.

PS8071.P68 1984   C810'.9'0054   C84-098733-1
PR9189.6.P68 1984

Published by Mosaic Press, P.O. Box 1032, Oakville, Ontario, L6J 5E9, Canada.

Published with the assistance of the Canada Council and the Ontario Arts Council.

Design by Deborah Thadaney
Realised by Doug Frank
Typeset by Speed River Graphics
Printed and bound in Canada

ISBN 0-88962-259-0 cloth
ISBN 0-88962-258-2 paper

MOSAIC PRESS:
In the United States: Flatiron Books, 175 Fifth Avenue, Suite 814, New York, N.Y. 10010, U.S.A.

In the U.K.: John Calder (Publishers) Ltd., 18 Brewer Street, London, W1R 4AS, England.

In New Zealand and Australia: Pilgrims South Press, P.O. Box 5101, Dunedin, New Zealand.

Contents

Acknowledgements

First, Marshall McLuhan; Irving Layton; Kenneth Sherman. Many have contributed with support, clarifications and disagreements, and they deserve special mention: George Sanderson promoted the essays and made invaluable suggestions; R.A. Paskauskas read the essays and offered criticism; Kate Hamilton, Peter Turner, and Fax, offered advice and encouragement, and typed early drafts; Shirley Brimacombe typed the final draft; Louise Oborne, Frauke Voss, and Tsigane, read, criticized, offered ideas. Others include: Howard Aster, Eric McLuhan, Brian Parker, Bradford Morrow, Joseph Amar, Georges Loranger, Jonathan Hart, Edward Pickersgill, Peter Martin, FLA and Kats (who made themselves available for commentary), Thadaney-Wittermann Design Communications, and last but not least, Deborah Thadaney, whose love and patience made it possible. I also acknowledge my thanks to Paul Savoie and Mirjana Lakich at the Canada Council for their support. Pieces, portions and ideas have appeared in *The Antigonish Review*, *The Boston Monthly*, *The Berkeley Monthly*, *The Bennington Review*, *Cross-Canada Writers' Quarterly*, *The Downtowner*, *Conjunctions*, *Blast 3*, and *Modern Drama*. I am especially indebted to the vigorous efforts of G.S. and everyone at *TAR*.

All quotations used represent excerpts only.

BWP, January 1984.

For BAP,
who also insisted that it be done.

I sincerely believe that the best criticism is the criticism that is entertaining and poetic; not a cold analytical type of criticism, which, claiming to explain everything, is devoid of hatred and love, and deliberately rids itself of any trace of feeling... As to criticism proper, I hope philosophers will understand what I am about to say: to be in focus, in other words to justify itself, criticism must be partial, passionate, political, that is to say it must adopt an exclusive point of view, provided always the one adopted opens up the widest horizons.

Baudelaire

Note

These essays are united by a common idea: they engage those contemporary Canadian writers and movements I consider important to myself and, I hope, to others concerned with writing and reading today. Certain questions dominate their direction. If as current critical axioms go, Canadian literature has matured, can it stand up to fresh scrutinies? Which writers give us the best strategies for understanding the world? Who uses language with authority? Who are the best enemies? As Wyndham Lewis and Elias Canetti have taught us: you must have an enemy if you are to develop a clear view of the age's attitudes and activities. These essays, then, do not form a non-evaluative study of selected Canadian writers: they are intended as an investigation, a reading, a reassessment, an exploration of the roads taken and not taken.

A word on the arrangement. The essays were written over three years and most were published separately, sometimes in a different form. The style of each piece was often dictated by the figure or fashion under consideration at the time. When necessary, I have supplied additional notes. I make no claims about trying to write a systematic commentary, so Alice Munro, Norman Levine, Earle Birney, and Mavis Gallant do not play the part that they should, and there is, perhaps unforgivably, no examination of playwrights. My references to French Canadian writers will also be sensationally limited; the scope of that material demands a separate volume.

Part One

Marshall McLuhan, the Put-on

ridentem dicere verum, quid vetat

Horace, *Satires,* **I.24**

Contradict yourself. In order to live, you must remain broken up.

Wyndham Lewis

In the autumn of 1978 I enrolled as a graduate student in English at the University of Toronto. I was entertaining hopes and, I'm afraid, the pose of being a writer, and was blithely unprepared for a juncture with Marshall McLuhan, a professor of Symbolist literature turned "media guru." It would be McLuhan's last year as a teacher, though I couldn't have known that. His famous Centre for Culture and Technology was on its way to oblivion, consigned there in a controversial move by University committees. McLuhan himself would be teaching his last "discovery," the Laws of the Media. There was, as well, a stroke impending, which would, in the most ironic way imaginable for one who had dedicated a lifetime to exploring communication, render him aphasiac, in virtual silence. He would retire in 1979; and on New Year's Eve morning, 1980, at the age of 69, he would be dead.

Marshall McLuhan was the author of *The Gutenberg Galaxy* and *Understanding Media,* a writer Susan Sontag had once included in a list with Nietzsche, John Cage, and Wittgenstein as indispensible to an understanding of the modern sensibility. He was, I still thought, identified with the mores and *mythos* and exuberance of the 1960s. He was a teacher and a *provocateur* and a celebrity and ... well, he was a lot of things, but nothing very exact. I had been too young to experience McLuhan's impact between 1965 and 1968. In the sullen seventies, ideas like "the medium is the message" had become a part of the *Zeitgeist* and were recognized as being uniquely "McLuhan". Despite that, I was not sure I knew what I was involving myself in.

At the English Faculty I tried to find out about the course McLuhan offered at the Centre. The outline in the University Calendar was bewilderingly brief: "English 1000, Media and Society", a one-sentence description and nothing, a half-empty page. I soon discovered that no one could tell me much more. Secretaries looked blank. "All I'm sure of," one said, "is that Dr. McLuhan doesn't begin teaching until October." An English professor tried to dissuade me: "I think most English students find that a year with Marshall is not of any particular value." Yesterday's savant. My curiosity, and nervousness, increased.

Even my peers were unaware of his presence on campus. I soon found myself imagining a room full of wide-eyed initiates listening to a decrepit cult-figure, or, worse, the aging "guru" lying on the floor, blathering on about Blake, The Beatles, and TV commercials.

However, I waited the extra weeks and finally on a grey Tuesday afternoon set out for the Centre. My difficulty was that I had only a vague idea as to where to look for it on the sprawling campus. And the name: *The Centre for Culture and Technology!* I was sure it would be a modern structure, perhaps following a design by Buckminster Fuller, with hordes of staff, students, and loitering sycophants, something that would measure up to the hyperbole of the name and the reputation of the man who ran it.

It turned out to be a small renovated coach house. It sat, as if forgotten, on a gravel lot behind a magnificent nineteenth century home, one of four old houses in a row. Each of these had been converted into classrooms that faced Queen's Park — with its trees like candelabra, joggers in sweat-suits, drunks, students, and politicians, northbound traffic on the roundabout, the back of the provincial legislature — a juxtaposition of Victorian turrets, towers, and spires with hard-edged modern shapes. A blue sign on Queen's Crescent East said:

CENTRE FOR CULTURE AND TECHNOLOGY
(NO. 39A AT BACK)

CENTRE FOR MEDIAEVAL STUDIES

EXPERIMENTAL
PHONETICS LABORATORY

Behind, to the east, sat St. Michael's College, the Catholic wing of the University, and the flashy Sutton Place Hotel. A service road stretched out back, littered with crates of trash.

The coach house itself resembled a tiny red brick barn. The wooden walk that led up through the parking lot was rotten and splintered. There were half-a-dozen small windows, like prison slits, and only the last one displayed a modest black-and-white sign.

The interior was even more unassuming. There were two rooms downstairs, the cramped reception area and offices of the administrative assistant, with its xerox machine, file cabinets, books, a black and white poster of Charlie Chaplin leaning on a cane, another of the Canadian Opera Company (1977), a cork bulletin board with cartoons and trivia, and signs ("If all else fails, read the instructions..."), a map of China, and more books.

The seminar room was a larger, green-carpeted area with a conference table, chairs (one with a sign that said: "Pierre Trudeau sat here!"), ratty couches giving off a slightly mouldy smell, a mural by René Cera and McLuhan's rowing oar from his days at Cambridge. On the west wall, Yeats' death mask was set beside a poster that said: "The first thing is to acquire *Perception*. Gain understanding tho' it cost you all you have. Proverbs."

Dismayed by these tawdry surroundings, I found a chair and sat down.

Twenty minutes later Marshall McLuhan stepped into the classroom and stood stiffly, as if in pain, looking pale and chewing gum. Glasses dangled from his hand.

"Is this it?" he said to no one in particular.

There were six in the class.

He lumbered to the front of the classroom and lounged on a polished walnut armchair, beside the paper-strewn table. He stared around the room, his eyes unfocussed. His suit was a mismatch of grey flannel and brown corduroy.

"Oh — well — " he spoke in a halting, reflective manner, "uh — this — is — uh," he pulled his chin down and shook his head, as if saying "no" in advance to a question. "Media and Society. I think...." he surveyed the nearly empty room, "we — uh — can begin.... now that there's *standing* room only." His eyes flashed; a grin appeared; his shoulders heaved in a way that would always, I found, accompany his appreciation of something comical.

McLuhan suddenly sprang out of his chair, poked his head out the doorway, and spoke to George Thompson, the administrative assistant, who sat at the desk in the reception room.

"So that's it?" McLuhan whispered. "I mean, uh, is this all that registered for the course?"

A mortified quiet ensued in the classroom; one or two shuffled papers and coughed. There was more hurried, indecipherable whispering.

"Oh," McLuhan said, his voice abrupt, flat.

He shut the door behind him. Over the door frame was the Shannon-Weaver model of communication:

Source — Transmitter — Signal — Receiver — Destination

Noise

"Well," he boomed. "I think this *is* it." He sat down again, picked up his glasses from where he had left them on the table. "So let's, uh, go over the reading list, shall we?"

He flipped through the papers on the table in front of him. The classroom was tense and receptive. In the early 1970s the students had burst into McLuhan's classes, commandeering the threadbare couch, sprawling on the floor, on metal chairs and cardboard boxes, leaning against the grey filing cabinets, backing up into the outer office and out the main door, sitting cross-legged and nearly cross-eyed at the teacher's feet, in their jeans, sweaters and suits. The Centre had had to order more chairs; regulate the flow; dismiss some and refuse others; as the class was "the right place" to be. Now it was nearly empty, as if a filtering process had occurred. Many of the cardboard boxes in the room contained remaindered copies of *The Executive as Drop-Out* and *From Cliché to Archetype*, McLuhan's later collaborative efforts.

The discussion of the booklist, however, took a spontaneous turn. He gave impromptu lectures on each book, never stayed on topic, then shifted to a discussion of cubism, and the revolution of multiple perspective. Apparently random statements were dropped: "Driving on a lineal highway is old hat. There's a kind of weaving now, a going in circles"; sudden puns: "Streakers are just a passing fanny"; aphorisms: "Terrorism is the normal condition of an acoustic age"; and allusions to Mallarmé and the typography of newspapers. He proceeded with astonishing speed.

By the time the two hour class rushed by in a display of jokes, judgements, references to his friendship with Ezra Pound and Lewis, and tantalizing ideas about media and modernism, I was hooked. As we filed out, McLuhan chatted with each person at the door, inviting us back next Tuesday, as if the course were a sort of friendly intellectual tea-party.

The list revealed in advance McLuhan's interdisciplinary approach to writing and teaching. It was the method of "interphase": subjects crossed and recrossed, leapt boundaries. I discovered, too, that McLuhan *always* filtered his perceptions through literature. A few students found themselves lost when he settled comfortably into Yeats, Joyce, Eliot, Pound, Baudelaire and Shakespeare, often reciting at length a favourite poem or quoting some awful pun from *Finnegans Wake*.

At some point in November I understood that a profound misconception had arisen over his name and concerns: the depth of his commitment to awakening audiences to the "Pure Present"; his literary bias, despite his predilection for oral teaching and dialogue; his emphasis on humour and satire; and how little he cared for the new technological environments. He had articulated "the speed of light" age, charting the effects of media "fallout" in *The Mechanical Bride* and *Understanding Media*, and studying the effect of print and the transition from the visual culture of books to the electronic, acoustic return to collective emotion in the work which is his major statement, *The Gutenberg Galaxy*. He had drawn attention to the force of new forms of communication, like TV, radio, the phonograph and film, and how they were displacing, but *not* replacing, the role of print. The later books, like *The Medium is the Message* and *War and Peace in the Global Village*, were derivative glosses of these earlier works, hastily written for a popular audience. *The Gutenberg Galaxy* remains an erudite, allusive, and at time opaque exposition on the configurations of this transitional period. McLuhan had allowed his image to be flashed over the world, his voice to emanate from the media he described, in a satirical mime of his argument. His questions about literacy were paradoxically conveyed through technology. Few *read* McLuhan. They came to know him through TV and radio. This was an ingenious, even comical, leap. That it was part of the question he asked about literacy, books, the written word, and the increasing dominance of electronic media eluded most observers. McLuhan himself became a mythic figure: and myth-making was, as he wrote, the central condition of the electronic media. Yet he also became for many a vulgarizer, a charlatan, an enthusiast of pop trash, an apologist for the new technologies. The conservative teacher and Catholic convert from Alberta (who did not even have a driver's license) became the visionary of the TV generation.

McLuhan occasionally wandered off on a ruminative tangent in class, wondering how someone could have composed a bumper-sticker declaring "McLuhan Reads Books" or how he came to be labelled the "media guru." "Anything beyond ordinary comprehension is guru-land," he snapped. McLuhan began as a literary man and remained one throughout even his most controversial stages. His work had begun at Cambridge in the study of Rhetoric and Dialectic, and the effect of manuscript culture and print on oral discussion, teaching, and thought, and later focussed on the writings of the Symbolists and the great modernists, Joyce, Lewis, Pound, Eliot and Yeats. As he insisted many times to us in class, it was only a small step from these writers, and their concerns with modes of communication, to the effects of electronic media and their social implications.

McLuhan believed he had come to an understanding of the modern world. He saw himself as a "mediator," a translator of the *Zeitgeist*'s manifestations into popular and poetic terms. His aim was to alert audiences: "In a period of rapid change you have to wake up. We are all sleepwalkers, but when you're changing from one element to the other, you must be completely awake."

There was a sense in which he allowed his message to be distorted. His refusal to make clear value judgements alienated ideologically inclined thinkers, particularly Marxists and most liberal humanists. He had said: "I want to understand everything, then neutralize it. Turn off as many buttons as you can. I am resolutely opposed to all change and innovation, but I am determined to understand what's happening." Yet as McLuhan himself taught, each electronic medium imposes its bias on the receiver *beyond* the rational value judgements of those users. The misunderstandings of his insights were, as he later realized with some horror, a sensational part of the mass-age.

However, McLuhan was addicted to antagonizing, spouting paradoxes, and carrying an idea to a frequently ridiculous extreme. This was in evidence during his Monday night seminars at the Centre, a so-called "free" night on which guest speakers came to participate in a dialogue. Some of these guests over the thirteen years of the Centre's existence had included Pierre Trudeau, Glenn Gould, John Lennon, Edward Albee, and Buckminster Fuller. They rarely got the chance to finish anything, as McLuhan would interrupt and the discussion would often assume a tone of high comedy, with cunning aphorisms being cuttingly exchanged.

One night in November McLuhan lounged unceremoniously in his armchair at the front of the seminar room with an associate sitting close by. An eager voice blurted:

"Dr. McLuhan, your colleagues think you're the most ignorant man on campus...."

"Yes, almost as ignorant as they are."

"But they think you pander in half-truths...."

"Now look," he sat forward, "a half-truth is an *awful* lot of truth! Most people never get that much!"

"But," the voice persisted, "you've only lived your whole life on a university campus."

"Well," McLuhan responded, "if you've lived on a university campus, you know a lot about stupidity. You don't have to go outside the university to understand the human condition."

There was laughter.

"You can't always recognize stupidity at first sight," he continued. "Or immaturity. Very few people go past the mental age of eleven now. It isn't safe! Why — they'd be alienated from the rest of the world!"

McLuhan was aware of this as a performance, his voice modulated to be loud and impressive. And on those Monday nights he was witty and cranky and cantankerous and egocentric to the point of megalomania. He could be flippant and authoritarian: "I'm tired of what you have to say," he once warned a garrulous businessman, "so I would appreciate it if you would just shut up." And yet in private, in his office, or at his home, he could be generous and solicitous; he would appear to forget your name, your presence, in fact everything, and then over lunch or tea or in conversation, be attentive to every word, eventually recalling to others something you said. His monologues and manuscripts were collaborations with everyone he conversed with: words, phrases, images and echoes found their way into the McLuhan manner and page, metamorphosed by his aphoristic, disjunctive style. He could be an elegant, old-world gentleman — as courtly as a Victorian lord — and an all-Canadian boor, chewing gum at public functions, cracking bad jokes, falling asleep and snoring during a guest's speech, seemingly lacking in social graces. It was all that which made him so eccentric — or, if you will, so ex-centric — an individual capable of assuming a multitude of guises, frequently in a perplexing array. I believe this is why he has had such an impact as a teacher. As his writing was notorious (indeed, considered scandalous) for its satirical undermining of linear argument, its off-hand remarks that concealed whole thoughts, its crabbed and harsh diction and heavily accented prose rhythms that forced the reader into a consciousness of the act of reading, so was his personality a "put-on," as elusive, allusive, and illusive as an ambiguous aphorism.

He prodded and provoked at those seminars, week after week, year after year, long after his spectacular emergence into TV fame, and long after his methods lost their glow of immediacy. He would speculate out loud ("The future of the book is the blurb. The unread book is the typical book of the time...."); riddle and lampoon ("The modern shower is a modern confessional — a sort of little box in which you stand up and 'come clean'...."); show an awesome disregard for facts ("The Beatles were four Irish lads...."); dismiss someone's work on the flimsiest basis — "would you trust a theory originated by someone named *Leakey*?" — and grandly state "I have no theories, only percepts." He said things that were so outrageous that you couldn't believe your ears: "When you go up in an airplane you actually begin to get small. This has been commented on by many parachutists." And then unexpectedly and casually he illuminated relations of thought: "Spelt from Sybil's leaves. Leaves of Grass. Hopkins. Whitman. Now, I wonder what relationship is there?" McLuhan enjoyed proceeding by analogical non-sequiturs; and his awareness of the poetic methods of Pound and Eliot gave his thinking an aesthetic shimmer, the penetrative power of a probe.

During the Monday night sessions he spun variations on his own ideas and aphorisms:

"At the speed of light there are no moving parts. At the speed of light, you don't have a body. On the telephone, on TV, on the radio, you are discarnate. This is the age of discarnate man. And without a body you can't be human. You can be God or devil, but you can't be human....

"This is the age of angelism, of angels and devils. Everybody is everywhere at once, by the speed of light transported to Japan, India, Brazil. We were once the victims of robotism. It is now angelism....

"Inflation is money travelling at the speed of light....

"Individualism, rationalism, and the nuclear family are helpless before the effects of electronic circuitry....

"In the electronic age we are living entirely by music...."

This was a method of social thought and a prose poetry reminiscent of the *Blast* manifestoes composed by Wyndham Lewis and Pound in 1914. McLuhan himself had written *Counterblast* in 1952, and then revised and expanded it in 1969 as a continuation of Lewis' polemical, analytical spirit. It was no wonder, though, that McLuhan alienated scholars and specialists, who resented and resisted his leaping, poetic manner. McLuhan took particular delight in irking academics, especially literary ones. His ultimate condemnation was to call a writer a "nineteenth century" thinker, caught in linear patterns of thinking and outmoded social values. It was not conservatism he criticized (for he was, as I had observed, a conservative man), it was their inability to understand what the modern world was ushering in. And, as he claimed, his "poster-aphoristic" style was parodic and fragmentary, arranged in "probes" and mosaics, to evoke the multiple processes of the radical present.

Critics retaliated by accusing McLuhan of using "the mimetic fallacy," Yvor Winter's phrase for the "aesthetic mistake" of employing a form which mimes the meaning of its own argument. McLuhan insisted that his major writings and public statements concerned "environments," the context of social change, what he called the "ground." "All my work is satire," he said. The collage of quotations, marginalia, and disjunctives was a parody of the "simultaneous, discontinuous" impact of mass media. The aphorisms were compressed philosophy. "The medium is the message" was ambivalent and unforgettable, like an advertising slogan, evoking the formal effect of any artifact on the human sensorium. The lesser known "user is content" referred to the receiver's perspective on the environment. (Which could be translated as: "You are the music while the music lasts.") *Everything* McLuhan did, in private, public, or in print, was shaped for maximum effect and involvement. "The job of the artist," he said (referring of course to himself), "is to command attention!"

It was, however, an article of his, long out of print, called "Catholic Humanism and Modern Letters" that finally clarified for me the roots and purpose of this work:

> The role of the Catholic humanist is to cultivate a more than ordinary reverence for the past, for tradition, while exploring every present development for what it reveals about man which the past has not revealed. To be contemporary in this sense is no mere snobbism, not a matter of faddishness. It is an arduous but rewarding business.... Speaking as a student of literature who has seen and experienced the undermining of formal literary study in our time by the new media of communication I think it is relevant to observe that it is especially the job of the Catholic humanist to build bridges between the arts and society today.[1]

To my knowledge McLuhan was never again as explicit, but his activities as a teacher, philosopher and satirist were a fulfillment of these pronouncements made in 1954.

* * *

In January, he called me into his office a few days after I had written a paper for him. He greeted me at the door of the second floor room, then sprawled on the tattered couch.

"Now, what did you want to see me about?"

"I thought you wanted to see me!"

"Oh yes. Quite right. About your paper."

He scrambled up and searched through a collection of essays. "Yes. Here it is."

He sat down, the informal manner dissolving into his magisterial tone and presence: the teacher. I was caught off guard, as I usually was by these quick shifts.

My essay explored the use of typography in Mallarmé and Charles Olson and in novelists like Beckett and Burroughs. The paper was not very good, yet what surprised me was the attack McLuhan launched on so-called literary post-modernism.

"Beckett is a diabolist," he said. "he sees life as something demonic, depraved. His reputation is out of proportion to the talent he has. Friend Burroughs, too. A nihilist. He loathes the world. Both of them cut the ground out of their work, leaving only abstracted figures. They've cut out their era and their audiences."

Their audiences. That was something so obvious for a writer that I had, of course, not considered it. For McLuhan, a literary work was not defined by theme or genre, but by audiences: the work achieved life only in relation to its effect on receivers and participants. This was, as McLuhan described it, Rhetoric.

He handed me a poem by Charles Olson and said: "Read it out loud."

When I finished, he remarked: "That was about as well as it could be read. But you shouldn't be reading these things. They're not good for you."

His critique extended to Malcolm Lowry — another "diabolist" — and even to Pound's *Cantos* — "a failure," he said. He questioned my reading of Eliot.

"Have you read Eliot's essays well?"

"Well, I think so — "

"Read them again. Mr. Eliot's comments on writing are percepts, not concepts. A percept only becomes a concept when replayed. Mr. Eliot was always concerned with trying to 'purify the dialect of the tribe' in order to communicate to and articulate his era. Olson and Burroughs have no awareness of compression or precision. They have lost contact with their audiences. An artist has to 'put-on' his audience. 'Hypocrite lecteur — mon semblable — mon frère.' He must understand his time, no matter what he sees."

We continued for over an hour, and I gradually understood that he was probing *me*, provoking and testing my responses. He criticized Abstract Expressionism — "It is all figure without ground" — and films — "The sounds of Star Wars are like the sounds one would hear on one of the levels of the Inferno" — propaganda techiques — "You ram something down your throat and you're bound to throw up" — and discussed finding ways of communicating in a world becoming increasingly passive and devoted to emotional, and not intellectual responses. Then as abruptly as he had begun, he stopped, and became again the kindly professor.

Walking out into the cold, I reeled from his shifts in manner and mood.

* * *

All this was part of McLuhan's "put-on." The "put-on" is a mask, a public role. It is not phoney, although it is artificial. The mask achieves its effect only with a listener or an audience; it substitutes a crowd for a mirror. The "put-on" is also a joke, a leg-pull, or a deliberate *put-off*. The advantage of this multiplicity over a conventional point of view, where the "I" is static, is its mobility. I think that is why he resisted every attempt to be consistent or categorized, and why he recklessly relished the unexpected, the contradictory, and the ridiculous. It was not just the professor as Possum: "People no longer feel limited to one personality under electronic circuitry," he said. He made himself the agent of his ideas: *the personality as probe.*

> He [the put-on artist] doesn't deal in isolated little tricks; rather, he has developed a pervasive style of relating to others that perpetually casts what he says into doubt. The put-on is an *open-end* form. That is to say it is rarely climaxed by having the "truth" set straight — when a truth, indeed, exists. "Straight" discussion, when one of the participants is putting the others on, is soon subverted and eventually sabotaged by uncertainty.[2]

McLuhan was *polytropos* — "skilled in many ways of contriving." Thus the blank incomprehension and confusion that some of his writing inspired was partially a result of his emphasis on personal presentation and performance. It has been suggested that there is as yet no accurate language for appraising the contribution of McLuhan,[3] and given the misinterpretation of his work, that would seem to be true. But the language and "put-on" was the man. Like his own idea of omnidirectional acoustic space, McLuhan came at you from every direction. So without some knowledge of how he worked, what he was, and the oral-satirical-critical tradition he was in, what he said does not have the same sensational context. It was a risk he was surely aware of: that he would be known as an orator and teacher, and through his impact on students and colleagues, and not purely as a writer.

During the next Monday night seminar, McLuhan interrupted a guest to say:

"A good teacher won't just offer his students a package, but a do-it-yourself kit. He will put him into a point of awareness. He will force him out of his previous modes of thinking. A good teacher saves you time."

* * *

At the end of the term, McLuhan held a final oral exam. When I finished mine in late June he asked me what my plans were. I told him I had decided not to go on for a Ph.D., and to devote myself to writing.

"You must be aware that you are taking a dangerous route," he said. "But you may be right: the future of the university is in some doubt as a vital institution. The U of T, for instance, is probably too large now to be of any real benefit. There is no contact between anybody. And the professors seem paralyzed in their inability to comprehend the world beyond its walls. You see, we may be entering a world where any kind of discipline is unbearable." He paused and added softly, "Nihilism is not a theory anymore, it's a condition."

He suggested lunch, so that we could go into detail in more congenial circumstances. Eating with him, however, was like having lunch with a random sampling of aphorisms from a selection of his books. Conversation varied between monologue (his) and monologue (mine). He again changed personae with alacrity: one moment, the pundit; the next, a paternal friend and punster; one moment, the man of letters; the next, the oracle, pronouncing portentous prophecies. He was at that time at work on *The Laws of the Media*.[4] Martin Heidegger came up:

"He sees technology as being a mystery, an occult form. He is solidly on the side of the irrational, which is acoustic. Technology for him has an autonomous existence. It is inhuman: a gift of the gods. Now, if I seriously believed technology was not man-made, I would simply drop-out... stop. I would not be in the least bit interested in technology if it were a mystery."

He ordered coffee, after the dessert, but before pouring it, he warned: "Never drink coffee after eating ice-cream. It cracks your teeth." He tucked his chin down and pondered. "You know — you must *never* go from hot to cool too quickly."

His face went blank as if I was not there, his mind on another thought.

Later, we left St. Michael's and returned to the Centre, where we spent a leisurely afternoon talking about his years at Cambridge with F.R. Leavis and I.A. Richards. As the day went on I noticed that he seemed to tire easily: his eyes were rheumy; his mannerisms became unusually languid; his thoughts came in spurts. It was as if he was slowing down right in front of me.

The conversation centred on the contemporary literary scene. "You may never know," he said, "what it was like to experience a true literary response in society. When a book was published by T.S. Eliot, there was a genuine response to it as literature. But writers aren't known that way today. They're media figures. They're known for anything but what they write. There is no literary audience now."

When I left, late in the afternoon, McLuhan stood at the door, looking drawn, and insisted that I come by the next week so that we could finish our conversation. For many reasons I did not get back to the Centre that summer. I have always regretted this. The lunch was the last time I saw him well.

* * *

McLuhan suffered a stroke in September. There was no public announcement. I discovered a few facts: McLuhan's classes had been cancelled, and Eric McLuhan, his eldest son, who was teaching full-time in Montreal, had taken over the running of the Centre's activities, leading the Monday night sessions.

That autumn, the assistant Dean of the School of Graduate Studies, Ernest McCullogh, announced that the Centre would be closed in June 1980, and that McLuhan would be retired. It did not take long for the newspapers, radio and TV to focus their attention on the coach house. Mail deluged the School of Graduate Studies. The letter page of the *Globe and Mail* was a storm-centre of conflicting opinions: "Not only is this move a slight to a lifetime achievement, it is also harmful to us all...." "The

Centre should have been shut down at least in 1977, if not earlier...." The *Globe and Mail* ran a headline: "Critics Give U of T Hard Knocks/Fans Rally To Support McLuhan"; and the *Toronto Star* published an editorial: *Understanding McLuhan Issue* ("The debate currently raging at the University of Toronto over the status of media analyst Marshall McLuhan and his Centre for Culture and Technology is something of a tempest in a TV tube....") There were rumours that Woody Allen, who had of course used McLuhan for a famous walk-on in "Annie Hall," had written to the U of T. The *Toronto Sun*, picking up on this, ran "Woody Gets the Message."

On the defensive, and I think taken by surprise, the School of Graduate Studies declared it would "review" its move to close the Centre. McLuhan was still unable to speak for himself. It had been by then publicly acknowledged that he had aphasia, the stroke affecting the speech patterns of the left hemisphere of the brain.

The struggle for the Centre's survival continued through the winter and spring of 1980. Public pressures and interest inevitably waned. McLuhan had improved sufficiently to allow a few appearances and work. Even with him being for the most part absent, the Centre still exuded his presence; the place was *placed* by his personality and work.

Which is not to romanticize the Centre's atmosphere. The aura of sycophancy which occasionally infested the place could be obnoxious; the Centre could (and did) draw bores, charlatans, and self-aggrandizers. There were often squads of literati and illuminati parroting McLuhanisms as if they were gospel; speaking in an incestuous jargon (cleverly called "shorthand") which frequently and alarmingly became a method of obfuscating ideas; exploiting McLuhan's reputation and intellectual reach for sometimes crudely financial ends; and using McLuhan's perceptions as an excuse to avoid individual perceptiveness.

That McLuhan had chosen to stay in Canada was an anomaly anyway. He could have established his Centre in a more sympathetic environment, perhaps in the United States. The Centre, as it was, was located off centre from the major area of the campus, isolated behind that Catholic library and the Victorian homes. His Centre had been a symbol of endurance against the conservative English faculty entrenched over at the King's Circle building. He faced enormous opposition in Canadian intellectual circles. He was respected, of course; but there was always the lingering sense of McLuhan as a subversive, a fake, a *poseur*, somehow — an *internationalist*.

Strangely, he preferred the antagonism. "You need the current going against you," he once said, "so that it's easier to steer a straight course." Even more curious, he liked his position as a Canadian, in what he saw as the serene and stolid backwoods of Toronto. "Canada is a country without an identity," he commented, "it is the country of interphase. We are rightly suspicious of any place which insists on a strong identity. Canada is a frontier, a perfect place for observation."

Now it looked as if he and his Centre were going to be victims of this Canadian parochialism and timidity.

On June 17, 1980, at six o'clock, the University of Toronto held a press conference to announce the decision that had been reached by the eight member committee concerning McLuhan's Centre. Their judgement was that it should be closed and a new program instituted. This was to be called the McLuhan Program in Culture and Technology, and would be governed by a board which would organize lectures and research. It was felt that without McLuhan directly involved, the place could not continue. No member or graduate of the Centre itself was on the Committee.

*   *   *

Not long after the announcement I returned to the Centre one afternoon. Eric McLuhan, George Thompson, and Carl Scharfe, a painter and friend of the McLuhan family, were packing boxes with books. McLuhan supervised the dismantling. Posters and drawings and maps and notes were taken down from the walls. Careful records were made of what was being stored and stacked in the large filing cabinets that had been sent over especially by the University. The move was unhurried and good-natured, with few shows of emotion.

Except for fleeting looks on McLuhan's face. When he passed through the seminar room, in a khaki coloured corduroy suit and a green plaid sports shirt, exasperation crept into his gestures and occasional speech. You could feel his silence. He walked about, as the books and papers were sorted and packed. He wrote on the blackboard, hummed to himself, his eyes livid, flashing and clear. All he could do was smile to himself. He stared or murmured and hummed and shook his head. "Boy oh boy oh boy," he mumbled. He stood back from the others, crossed his arms, and registered that wry look of loss and surprise, humour and incapacity.

Suddenly McLuhan walked over to where George Thompson was rolling a large poster. "No, no, no." He grabbed it.

"What is it, Marshall?" Thompson asked.

"No," McLuhan repeated. He unrolled the poster and placed it against the bare wall.

Eric and Carl Scharfe gathered to see what Marshall was doing. The poster was an enlarged black and white still from a Marx Brothers movie. It showed Groucho, Chico, Harpo and Zeppo leaning against each other, wearing looks of tired amazement after a day of confusion.

"You want that up, dad?" Eric asked.

"Yes." McLuhan was laughing.

"OK, it stays there until we're out."

George Thompson took a roll of tape and fixed the poster to the wall.

There were phone calls throughout the day, callers with enquiries as to the future and details of the so-called McLuhan program. Friends and acquaintances phoned and visited and talked.

Toward evening Eric McLuhan worked alone at the long cluttered table in the dimly lit seminar room. McLuhan had gone home.

"It's too late to be bitter," he said. "The Dean wants to give us an extra week or two to move. Don't rush, he said. But I don't agree. Pack it up. Get out. Get it over with. Then we can start again."

* * *

I had time to remember what the Centre had been like and my encounters with McLuhan. I would see him again in different circumstances, but I gradually realized how McLuhan's coach house had been a place of handing on. It had housed and shaped a thousand similar experiences. Something of McLuhan himself, however, remained maddeningly complex, as if I had glimpsed only the surfaces of his "put-on," like a message not clearly understood, a provocative and demanding ambiguity that would, I guessed, stay with me for a long time. I thought of these lines of Eliot's:

We had the experience but missed the meaning,
And approach to the meaning restores the experience
In a different form, beyond any meaning
We can assign to happiness.

I went back to the Centre in late September. There were dead leaves in the driveway. The building was dark. The windows were curtained; there were no sounds of typewriters or telephones. The files and papers and books and mementoes had all, at last, been packed up and scattered to McLuhan's home and other places. The small blue sign was still out front: *Centre for Culture and Technology*. There were, however, no other signs to inform you of what it was that had once been there.

(1981)

Fear of Fryeing:
Northrop Frye and the Theory
of Myth Criticism

"La théorie c'est bon, mais ça n'empêche pas d'exister."
Charcot

A man might be clothed in armour so complicated and elaborate, that to the inhabitant of another planet who had never seen armour before, he might seem like some entirely impersonal and omnipotent mechanical force. But if he saw the armour running after a lady, or eating tarts in the pantry, he would realize at once that it was not a god-like or mechanical force, but an ordinary human being extraordinarily armed.
T.E. Hulme

I

Northrop Frye's name acts like a magic talisman in the mouths of literary scholars, critics, and English students. Its mere mention invokes a writer-philosopher of such magnitude that only genuflection is appropriate. He has been called Canada's greatest cultural historian, "the visionary critic," and as Murray Krieger writes in "Northrop Frye and Contemporary Criticism — Ariel and the Spirit of Gravity": "he has had an influence — indeed an absolute hold — on a generation of developing literary critics greater and more exclusive than that of any one theorist in recent history."[1] Even the reading public, who would never wade through such weighty tomes as *The Anatomy of Criticism* and *The Great Code*, think of Frye as a deified genius.

How a professor of literature came to project that aura of authority is a fascinating phenomenon. Yet few writers and readers seem capable of summarizing what Frye thinks — that is, what his theories are and what they mean.

This is not Frye's fault. He is generally forthright, rarely outrageous, and committed to expressing his argument in explicit prose. A reader's impression of, say, *The Educated Imagination* or *The Modern Century*, is likely to be of a modest professor monotonously explicating a theory and various patterns in culture. You would hardly expect the electricity or an opinionated mind from what seems... so flat.

First appearance aside, Frye has a coherent theory and a cogent critical stand. His theory consists of a conception of a single unified myth which pervades all of literature: the myth of identity. He describes the permanent recurring forms of literary history and stresses the roles of convention and tradition in shaping poetry and prose-fiction. Frye's contribution is that of the establishment of a "scientific criticism," of the detached critic who studies these structures without regard to their moral effect or quality, their biographical reference, and power as agents of change in a reader's perception. Frye is, as he claims, a classifier of knowledge, a maker of systems which identify a poetic universe informed by transcendental *schemata*, an ideal world of the imagination which the "true" critic teaches us to contemplate.

To comprehend this, we must look to *The Anatomy of Criticism* for the theory, and to distillations and collections like *The Educated Imagination*, *The Stubborn Structure: Essays on Criticism and Society*, *The Well-Tempered Critic*, *The Critical Path*, and *Spiritus Mundi*. His books on William Blake, *Fearful Symmetry*, and the Bible, *The Great Code*, cannot concern me deeply. This is admittedly a limitation, as Frye's erudition in these works is impressive and challenging. His clear prose style, extensive classical reading and rigorously organized research are infinitely preferable to the mangled language and obliquities of Jacques Derrida and his kind. It is, however, the ramifications of his theory and the near deification of Frye as a thinker that I intend to engage here.

II

The Anatomy of Criticism (1957) lays the foundation for a new kind of criticism — archetypal or myth criticism. In the "Polemical Introduction", Frye dismisses virtually every other type of criticism with a sort of tolerant, half-amused snort. He acknowledges on the first page that his book is "a synoptic view of the scope, theory, principles, and techniques of literary criticism." (*The Anatomy of Criticism*, p. 3). Which is to say, the book is a "pure" critical analysis of other critical techniques. Frye follows with a defense of criticism as an essential creative enterprise. He derides those artists who consider criticism to be parasitic, secondary. This would be comprehensible coming from a novelist, poet, or playwright, for the great critics of literature have consistently been artists, like Dr. Johnson, Coleridge, Matthew Arnold, Oscar Wilde, Henry James, T.S. Eliot, and Ezra Pound. However, it has been a peculiar aspect of the late twentieth century that the "pure" literary critic has appeared. Frye is neither poet, novelist, nor playwright, so he gives to his books an air of detachment which can only come from scholarship. He is a philosopher of criticism; he is *the critic* as artist. Frye continues, in his "Polemical Introduction," to shower contempt on anti-academic ranting, as he establishes the concept of the "pure" critic as creator.

Now, almost no one denies that criticism is creative. As Frye points out, a civilization without its critics is imperiled. A critic's job as interpreter and evaluator, as a cultural seismograph, can be significant. The serious critic can be a transmitter of humane values, of focussed perception, and of vital traditions. But this is not what Frye has in mind when he begins to exalt the "pure" critic as artist. Frye's unique conceit is to declare that the true critic's job is to create a system whose object it is to study art. That is, we cannot see art *directly* ("Poetry is a *disinterested* use of words: it does not address a reader directly...." *The Anatomy of Criticism*, p. 4); we can only see through the eyes of criticism.

Thus Frye writes:

> Once we admit that the critic has his own field of activity, and that he has autonomy within that field, we have to concede that criticism deals with literature in terms of a specific conceptual framework. (*The Anatomy of Criticism*, p. 6)

In order to create this "framework," the first step for the critic is to

> ...get rid of meaningless criticism, or talking about literature in a way that cannot help to build up a systematic structure of knowledge. This includes all the sonorous nonsense that we so often find in critical generalities.... and other consequences of taking a large view of an unorganized subject. It includes all lists of the 'best' novels or poems or writers, whether their particular virtue is exclusiveness or inclusiveness. It includes all casual, sentimental and prejudiced value-judgements, and all the literary chit-chat which makes the reputations of poets boom and crash in an imaginary stock exchange. (*The Anatomy of Criticism*, p. 18)

The stripping away of critical fads would allow a coherent body of knowledge about literature to appear. If literature cannot be known directly — for all immediate personal experience is a reflection of taste — then criticism becomes the primary instrument of knowledge.

The dismissal of unique and therefore unclassifiable experience, is fundamental to Frye's reasoning. He says:

> In the history of taste, where there are no facts, and where all truths have been, in Hegelian fashion, split into half-truths in order to sharpen their cutting edges, we perhaps do feel that the study of literature is too relative and subjective ever to make any consistent sense. But as the history of taste has no organic connection with criticism, it can easily be separated. Mr. Eliot's essay *The Function of Criticism* begins by laying down the principle that the existing monuments of literature form an ideal order among themselves, and are not simply collections of the writings of individuals." (*The Anatomy of Criticism*, p. 18)

Here we have a host of assumptions about taste, truth, subjectivity, and the individuality of a single work and its place in Tradition. Eliot's influence on Frye is enormous, and I will come back to this shortly. What Frye is suggesting is that literary criticism is (or should be) a pseudo-scientific approach that operates *beyond* taste, value-judgements, and the uniqueness of an artist and his work. As Frye writes earlier in the introduction: "The development of such a criticism *would fulfil the systematic and progressive element in research by assimilating its work into a unified structure of knowledge, as other sciences do.*" (*The Anatomy of Criticism*, p. 11, emphasis mine)

Later in the "Polemical Introduction," Frye rejects the notion that art teaches values — "positive values... goodness...." (*The Anatomy of Criticism*, p. 27) He declares that criticism can only become "systematic" if there is something *in* literature which allows this. In the poems, plays and novels of western literature is a hidden deep structure to be identified and categorized by the critic. This is the mythic bedrock of the literary artifact. Literature is an order of words; art creates myths; and criticism should become the vehicle for identifying these enduring mythic shapes which explain the universe.

So, from Frye's introduction, can we surmise what kind of criticism he wants to create? Let us allow Frye to answer in a passage from *The Well-Tempered Critic* (1963):

> The fundamental act of criticism is a disinterested response to
> a work of literature in which all one's beliefs, engagements,
> commitments, prejudices, stampedings of pity and terror, are
> ordered to be quiet. We are now dealing with the
> imaginative, not the existential, with the "let this be," not
> with "this is," and no work of literature is better by virtue of
> what it says than any other work. (*The Well-Tempered Critic*,
> p. 140)

Frye's critic would be a cool analyst, reluctant to express personal
convictions about the value of one work over another. All
literature would be his ground: Chaucer and Dylan Thomas exist
in "a simultaneous order." The critics would examine the
recurring forms of the imagination, the archetypes. Why? Because
knowledge, purged of human prejudice and taste, must be
objectively conveyed to students, teachers, and "the common
reader." The critic moves into cultural history (Tradition) in
order to see how these mythic structures have cohered. The
touchstones, the ruling patterns, would be taken from the Bible
(which provides "the great code"), Homer, and Ovid's *Meta-morphosis*.

    The Anatomy of Criticism thus unfolds as a systematic analysis of
modes (tragic, comic), symbols, and myths. In the chapter on
"mythos," a key one, Frye echoes Spengler, Vico, Joyce, and
Yeats by introducing a fourfold structure of mythical recurrence
based on the four seasons. We quickly observe that Frye's *Anatomy*
itself is arranged around a four-part division of essays. All this is
part of an elaborate, dispassionate system, the work of the kind of
critic that the "Polemical Introduction" has called for. On every
page we encounter that same impersonal, classifying scientific
spirit, methodically creating a huge timeless structure. By
*de*moralizing the effect of a particular work (so that, for example,
by taking the *literal* hell from Rimbaud's "Une Saison En Enfer,"
the poem becomes a representative of a descent or apocalyptic
myth) every work becomes part of a monolithic system. And this
system is shapely, stately and grand, a pseudo-art object that
requires sustained contemplation. *The Anatomy of Criticism* presents
the study of art in an ideal vacuum, a condition of stasis.

    The "Tentative Conclusion" again expresses Frye's prefer-
ence for archetypal criticism. Literature, he says, being an order of
words, creates "verbal universes" — imaginative models, like
Prospero's isle of magic and masques in *The Tempest*. Mathematical models and models made of words are not really different.

Each provides a way of organizing a vision of the world in a myth. (Thomas Kuhn's *The Structure of Scientific Revolutions*, which advances the concept of paradigms, is relevant here.)

Frye's last remarks in *The Anatomy* are worth quoting because they reveal what Frye believes to be the calling of the "pure" critic:

> If I have read the last chapter of *Finnegans Wake* correctly, what happens here is that the dreamer, after spending the night in communion with a vast body of metaphorical identifications, wakens and goes about his business forgetting his dream, like Nebuchadnezzar, failing to use, or even to realize that he can use, the "keys to dreamland." What he fails to do is therefore left for the reader to do, the "ideal reader suffering from an ideal insomnia," as Joyce calls him, in other words the critic. Some such activity as this of reforging the broken links between creation and knowledge, art and science, myth and concept, is what I envisage for criticism. (*The Anatomy of Criticism*, p. 354)

Despite his claim that he is a theorist of disinterested criticism, this has a mystical-prophetic tone which invokes the image of the critic as magus, as a great synthesizer.

The elevation of the "pure" literary critic is one of Frye's most important conceits. He insists that the artist is not the best guide to his own work, or, for that matter, to anyone else's. The artist creates documents which the *real* critic inspects. He writes in *The Educated Imagination* (1963) that: "It's not surprising if writers are often rather simple people, not always what we think of as intellectuals, and certainly not always any freer of silliness or perversity than anyone else." (p. 9) Later, in an indirect attack on the Romantic image of the artist as hero, Frye says "the poet as a person is no wiser or better a man than anyone else. He's a man with a special craft of putting words together, but he may have no claim to our attention beyond that." (p. 29) Finally: "...you certainly wouldn't turn to contemporary poets for guidance or leadership in the twentieth-century world." (p. 7) And with that Frye dismisses Yeats, Pound, Eliot and Lawrence for their "aberrant" politics.

For Frye, an artist is either simple, confused, or unspeakably sneaky. The writer is at best when conventions and myths are controlling him. "That's why so much of a writer's best writing is or seems to be involuntary," he says. You can see Frye's debt to

T.S. Eliot, for this is Eliot's artist as a "transforming catalyst" surfacing in another guise, only now as "the naïve catalyst." What Frye is saying is that artists are inferior to the professional critic as an interpreter of a work. Granted, some writers are awkward on the subject of their craft; but Frye's implied description of the artist as an elemental *naïf* is straight propaganda. It is part of his strategy for recreating the role of the critic, for making *him* the authority on the literary work.

This is where the notion of Frye as "the visionary critic" comes from. The literary critic, after Frye, becomes the mighty mediator, the giant who holds the "keys to dreamland." With *The Anatomy of Criticism*, Frye's ambitions and range appear to put him into a class by himself. Hence the intimidating quality of his presence and declarations; hence the comment from Marshall McLuhan: "Norrie is not looking for his place in the sun. He *is* the sun."[2]

In subsequent critical books, Frye moves on to cultural history and theories of educating the imagination. He elaborates upon his concepts of "the poetic universe," "the verbal universe," the role of the artist and critic, and the aims of literary study. In *The Well-Tempered Critic*, *The Educated Imagination*, and *The Stubborn Structure: Essays on Criticism and Society*, we find the conception of the ideal "isle" of art, separate from the "real world," a sort of interior theatre that has "nothing" to say about life. Here is Frye's distinction between science and art, and the idealistic basis he invokes, from *The Educated Imagination*:

> Science begins with the world we have to live in, accepting its data and trying to explain its laws. From there, it moves towards the imagination: it becomes a mental construct, a model of a possible way of interpreting experience. The further it goes in this direction, the more it tends to speak the language of mathematics, which is really one of the languages of the imagination, along with literature and music. Art, on the other hand, begins with the world we construct, not with the world we see.... *one starts with the world as it is, the other with the world we want to have.* (p. 6, emphasis mine)

The theory of the imagination unfolds logically from the "ideal critic" and "ideal system" of *The Anatomy of Criticism*. The imagination is "the power of constructing possible models of human experience. In the world of the imagination, anything goes that's imaginatively possible, but nothing really happens" (*The Educated Imagination*, p. 5). Again, if the artist's experiences and life are unimportant, then we must look to the work, and the work of art exists only in "the head," a world within a world. "...literature," Frye writes, "has no consistent connexion with ordinary life, positive or negative." (p. 39) And: "The world of literature is a world where there is no reality except that of the human imagination" (p. 40).

This is "the poetic universe" where anything is possible because everything is a fiction. Reading is a process of learning how to comprehend and use that Utopian "placc" which exists outside the whims and winds of reality. The true critic must therefore become an educator. For what literature does — if it "does" anything — is to refresh or inspire our sense of the ideal. Thus the student must learn how to use his dormant imaginative powers. "Education is concerned with two worlds," Frye writes in his essay "The Instruments of Mental Torture," "the world that man lives in and the world he wants to live in...."[3] Education shapes and trains the imagination to view this interior theatre, the world we "want to live in," not the world "that is."

To summarize: the imagination becomes the playground of the educated intellect. Art is ruled by conventions and myths. The artist is a catalyst for these. The critic is the all-important intercessor because we have no direct experience of art. Art is not a part of life; it exists only in the imagination. The importance of art is to teach us how to resist "stock responses." Value-judgements and moral perspectives are irrelevant. The only truth is poetic truth, which is not Truth, but a fiction *about* life. Art is neither a mirror nor a lamp; it is an artificial, self-inferring "isle."

The issue of value-judgements is worth further examination. In an essay in *The Stubborn Structure* (1970) called "Value-judgements," Frye states, in what is surely the first recorded case of Frye almost losing his temper (and slipping momentarily from the impersonal to the personal), these opinions:

> I have nothing new to say on this question... (p. 66) One cannot pursue that study [of literature] with the object of arriving at value-judgements, because the only possible goal of study is knowledge.... (p. 66) The literary scholar has *nothing to do with sifting out what will be less rewarding to experience*.... (p. 67, emphasis mine) It is because I believe in the value of literary scholarship that I doubt that value-judgements have a genuine function in acquiring it. (p. 71)

Evaluations and revaluations do not exist for the "true" critic. The pursuit of his study should only be "knowledge." The moral effect of this knowledge on experience is not important.

Thus we can see why Frye has been called the scholar's scholar, for his work is a massive apologia for the scholar's task, a *summa* for the detached academic exegete. Indeed, the greater portion of Frye's writings are directed at teaching, and so, we find, his greatest influence has been in school systems.

III

I have watched Northrop Frye teach: a diminutive portly gentleman slips quietly, with no fanfare, into a classroom in Victoria College at the University of Toronto. His face is round, pale, and puffy; his wire-frame glasses are thick; his checkered tweed suit is wrinkled. Professor Frye is the incarnation of what was once known as the browner: the studious, withdrawn, and invariably brainy student. The professor shambles up to the front of the quiet classroom — which is filled to capacity — and places his battered briefcase on the table. He removes his glasses, opens a small felt case, takes out another pair, which he sets on his nose. He peers around and clears his throat. The students crane forward in their desks, pens ready. The object of study today is Eliot's "The Waste Land." The class begins. Frye's lecturing manner is gentle, soft-spoken, informal. It soon becomes obvious, though, as the class proceeds, that this is a *lecture*, and not a dialogue.

("What seems not to have been noticed," Frye writes in "The University and Personal Life," "is the fact that there is really no such thing as 'dialogue.' Just as some children try to behave like heroes and heroines in the stories they read, so 'dialogue' is a literary convention taken to be a fact of life. The literary convention comes from Plato, and we notice how clearly aware Plato is of the fact that unstructured discussion is a collection of solipsistic monologues.")[4]

Frye is droll and encyclopaedic during his lecture, drawing on obscure references, sorting out sources. Phrases pile up in perfect paragraphs. He pauses. Questions are invited. He listens politely, and replies. Dialogue is not prolonged. The lecture resumes.

("Nothing *happens* in Plato," Frye writes in that same essay on the University in *Spiritus Mundi*, "until one person, generally Socrates, assumes control of the argument and the contributions of the others are largely reduced to punctuation.")[5]

After an elaboration of the mythological framework behind Eliot's poem, Frye discusses "The Waste Land," beginning with the "Notes" and not the poem. He spends over twenty minutes explicating the allusions, the references to other books, particularly Fraser's *The Golden Bough*. When a lone voice from the class remarks that Eliot had once dismissed the "Notes" as a skit — and it is relevant to note that Ezra Pound, in his editorial midwifery of "The Waste Land," stated that the "Notes" were a mistake, moving the poem toward scholasticism and away from public utterance, distracting the reader from the work's immediacy — Frye dismisses Eliot's comment. Frye replies that the "Notes" demonstrate the mythological structure that Eliot was working in.

The professor continues with a discussion of how this structure is a fiction created to protect ourselves against life, what he calls our "verbal insulation." He comments: "I don't think reality is anything human beings should have any business with. Our whole life consists in a choice of illusions." Later he says: "The world of animals and vegetal life does not exist for man except as part of imaginative constructs."

Schematic diagrams appear on the chalkboard. Mysterious, almost mathematical designs take shape. Codes; patterns.

("One great advantage of teaching literature systematically," Frye writes in *On Teaching Literature*, an influential booklet intended for teachers and schools, "is that it then turns out to be a structure, like mathematics or science, and the memory work involved becomes a good deal simpler when there is something to hook on to.")[6]

There are reflective gaps in his lecture. He sits down and stares, his head slightly inclined, drumming his fingers on the table; then coughing again, he stands, and pursues another strand of thought. After class he again listens to questions from students. The others file out, their notebooks full.

* * *

"Frye's effect on Canada's and America's educational institutions," writes Wayne Grady in "The Educated Imagination of Northrop Frye," "... is profound. His work has permeated the teaching and learning of literature, and, indeed, the very fabric of our culture."[7]

So rhapsodizes a typical commentator, repeating what has been said a thousand times and never questioned. A "detached" teacher, of course, could not possibly mislead students or offer a system of criticism which would have any special effect, "positive or negative." And since Frye has eschewed value-judgements, moral evaluations, personal, political, or spiritual comments, there is (clearly) "nothing" at stake. Except pure education — *knowledge.*

Thus, as Mr. Grady happily points out, Frye's system of myth criticism has indeed infused a generation of teachers and critics, who by mimicking the master's manner have been sarcastically dubbed "small Fryes." It has been quipped that most of the Faculty of English at the University of Western Ontario are former Frye students. All this has been understandable, for there has been little opposition. Books like *The Bush Garden, Fearful Symmetry, The Modern Century,* and *A Study of English Romanticism,* are routinely assigned to credulous classes. Frye himself has sat on such important cultural committees as the Canadian Radio-Television Commission (1968-1977). Margaret Atwood, Dennis Lee, and Eli Mandel are former students, and each of their critical books bear the undeniable imprint of Frye's thinking. And obviously he has been involved in many colloquia devoted to examining teaching techniques. It is easy to see why Frye has had such an influence. His books are a teacher's delight. They are organized, precise, ambitious, subtly conservative, ostentatiously erudite. Their calm soothing surfaces have a reassuring quality, and for teachers who have not bothered to do their own research, it all seems *right.* The potentially upsetting aspects of literature — its active penetrations into how we live, its insistence on *seeing* and *hearing* — are softened and even quietly defused. So for example, we find Professor Frye writing the following declaration in *On Teaching Literature* (1972):

> Very often literary models in school books are organized by content, by what they say about love or time or death or what not. When well done, such an approach may overlap with the present one: putting poems on spring together is to some extent arrangement by content too. But the approach of this program also provides a containing form for the themes: love and death are not taken as real classifying principles, but as aspects of literary genres, such as comedy and tragedy. This avoids the danger of classifying literature by what it says, and so making literary works into documents illustrating various Noble Notions. It thus avoids the moralizing of literature, of treating it as a collection of allegories of something else.... (*On Teaching Literature*, p. 12)

Which is a statement notable not only for its sleep-inducing effect, but for its elimination of the moral dimension of art with hardly a whimper.

Frye does insist that the goal of literary study is the unfettering of the imagination from what he calls, in various essays, "the stock response." Goaded by galling critics who have accused him of everything from arrogant indifference and obscurantism to proto-fascistic theorizing, he formulates the idea that literature teaches us "the myth of freedom" and "the myth of concern":

> If he [the teacher] is teaching literature, he is trying also to teach the ability to be aware of one's imaginative social vision, and so to escape the prison of unconscious social conditioning. Whatever he is teaching, he is teaching some aspect of the freedom of man. (*On Teaching Literature*, p. 29)

A noble sentiment, although hardly new. It is also so vague as to constitute little as a tangible end. If the "freedom of man" is the objective, what sort of freedom does Frye have in mind? Freedom from "stock responses" and "clichés" is not the answer, for we all use stock responses and clichés to some extent. It could be charged that Frye himself has solidified his system to such a point that *it* has become a stock response; and think of what James Joyce and William Carlos Williams have done with clichés. Clichés and stock responses, though a way of cheapening intellectual life, are not necessarily the roads to totalitarianism or decadence. It is not surprising that what Frye has to say on this subject is no more than glibly reassuring, for the only freedom his teaching and theorizing propose is the freedom of the imagination to range over the artificial landscapes of art.

IV

The origins of Frye's theories are easy to trace. In 1865, Matthew Arnold wrote in his essay, "The Function of Criticism at the Present Time" that a kind of criticism was needed which would be a "disinterested endeavour to learn and propagate the best that is known and thought in the world."[8] Faced with critical writings which often seemed to serve obviously political ends, and whose standards were not of the highest order, Arnold imagined a mode which would raise intellectual standards and pursue the best throughout literary history. "Real criticism," Arnold wrote, "is essentially the exercise of... *curiosity*,"[9] although it is secondary to art itself.

The standard of objective curiosity was not met in Arnold's time. However, we can hear in his call the implicit demand for scrupulous organization, for a systematic way of approaching "the best," for a critic who would avoid "practicality" and study knowledge "for its own sake."

Add to this Oscar Wilde's marvellously mannered essay, "The Decay of Lying" (1891):

> If Nature had been comfortable, mankind would never have invented architecture, and I prefer houses to open air. In a house we all feel of the proper proportions. Everything is subordinated to us, fashioned for our use and our pleasure.[10]

And:

> My own experience is that the more we study Art, the less we care for Nature. What Art really reveals to us is Nature's lack of design, her curious crudities, her extraordinary monotony, her absolutely unfinished condition.[11]

Here Wilde is subversively extolling the virtues of "artifice," "the artificial," the imaginative ability to create images ("image": "imagine": "to conceive": Latin, imaginari, "to picture to one's self, a likeness"). The authentic artist is a maker, not a mirror. Wilde's world is the domain of the ideal (the mental image).* He rejects the verisimilitude of novelists like Zola and George Eliot, dismissing their techniques of attentive historical realism. The "lying" of Wilde's title is "the supreme fiction," the ability to create an interior world out of language, superior to reality.

Recall Frye: "The world of literature is a world where there is no reality except that of the imagination." (*The Educated Imagination*, p. 40) Recall that Frye invokes Arnold's name on the first page of *The Anatomy of Criticism*. Recall, too, Frye's emphatic rejection of didacticism and the values of realistic *seeing*. Frye heeded Arnold's call, while annexing Wilde's notion of the transcendence of art. Throw in a streak of the Aristotelian mania for categorization, and Frye's theory begins to impend.

---

* I am using "ideal" in its strict philosophical sense. "Ideal" meaning that only the mental is knowable, and therefore reality is essentially spiritual or mental. Cf. Berkeley. Indeed, Frye's debt to Berkeley, via Blake, is enormous.

The other influences are obvious: they are William Blake, Carl Jung, and T.S. Eliot. The Jungian archetypes and his theory of the collective unconscious provided Frye with the concept of eternal myths forming an enduring construct in the imagination. However, the debt to Jung runs deeper, for Jung, like Frye, also had a concept of art as a "dream-state" that exists outside the order of events. Eliot's essays "Tradition and the Individual Talent" and "The Function of Criticism" are important to Frye's theories, particularly in his ideas about "simultaneous history" (all art is now; art never improves), and the disengagement of the critic from personal concerns.

The anomaly is William Blake. *Fearful Symmetry* (1947) is one of Frye's most respected books. His thought has been influenced by Blake's vision of the imagination as a force that operates outside of time and space and unites with God. (It is worth remembering that a hidden bias in Frye's writings is his religious view, which is Protestant and quasi-mystical. Hence *The Great Code*.) Yet the Blake which emerges from *Fearful Symmetry* is a strange Blake, a Poet for Poetry's Sake, creating his systems with the purpose of teaching the reader how to understand myth and allegory. "I must Create a System or be enslav'd by another Man's," Blake writes in an oft-quoted line from *Jerusalem*, a line which underlies Frye's aspirations. However, Frye's Blake is not a prophet-revolutionary, not the author of "The Marriage and Heaven and Hell," not the Blake who wrote "To Generalize is to be an Idiot," not the Blake who appears in Mark Schorer's *William Blake: The Politics of Vision* or David Erdman's *Blake: Prophet Against Empire*. Suddenly Blake becomes a poet recreating a new coherent mythology and articulating a theory of the imagination as detached union with God!

There are other resonances in Frye's thought of course, but the foregoing are the important ones. Returning again to Wilde, this exchange from "The Critic as Artist" recalls the intended end of Frye's teachings and theories of criticism:

> Gilbert: ... Contemplation... in the opinion of the highest culture it is the proper occupation of man.
> Ernest: Contemplation?
> Gilbert: Contemplation...
> Ernest: We exist, then, to do nothing?
> Gilbert: It is to do nothing that the elect exist. Action is limited and relative. Unlimited and absolute is the vision of him who sits at ease and watches, who walks in loneliness and dreams.[12]

V

My objections to Frye's theories centre on his emphasis on theoretical systems, his refusal to incorporate the individual (and thus the unpredictable and unique), his dismissal of value-judgements, and finally the relative passivity, the inertness, of his undertaking.

Theoretical systems in literary criticism are dangerous ground if they do not sharpen the reader's awareness of the text, and of the text's relationship to life. Frye cherishes order, coherence and schematic diagrams which provide convenient handles on the sprawling, apparently undisciplined, mass of literature. He is continually offering theoretical packages which have developed from years of devoted reading, packages which offer keys to "stubborn structures," "great codes," "critical paths." Nevertheless, these packages cannot conceal the limitations of conceptual thought and the neutered role Frye assigns to the serious writer, critic, and reader.

There is a *choice* here: it is that of "theory" as opposed to perception. Etymologies are useful. Theory comes from the Latin "theoria" and the Greek θεωρία , meaning a contemplation, a speculation. "Theory" is also related to "theatre" — a place for seeing. The Greek root θέα means spectacle (there are derivative words like speculate and spectacular). Now, "perception." "Perceive" comes from "percipere" (Latin), meaning to apprehend. "Apprehendere," also Latin, means "to lay hold of," *to seize*. It should be apparent that "theory" suggests something static, while "perception" suggests action, "a taking hold of." The world of Frye's criticism is "theoria"; that of the artist and vital criticism is "percipere." Given this understanding of the emphasis Frye places on "theoria," it should not surprise anyone to realize that there is not a single major novelist, poet or playwright who has been influenced by him. As I have been showing, the only public Frye is aware of is composed of teachers, students, and writers of articles for scholarly journals ("consumers of literature," he calls them), and even then he appears to be unaware of what is at stake by enjoining these "consumers" to ignore reality, moral evaluations, historical and biographical references, and value-judgements.

For again: what kind of criticism does Frye want? What remains after his *Anatomy*? What would be the role of the "true" Frye critic? What could be the result of his teachings and theorizings?

Frye so neatly annihilates other forms of criticism in the "Polemical Introduction" to *The Anatomy of Criticism* that a reader unfamiliar with these might never realize what is being rejected. You soon see that out goes F.R. Leavis and his revaluations of individual novelists and poets; I.A. Richards' investigations of the relationship between a poetic text and the reader's perception of it in *Practical Criticism*; Pound's essays on behalf of his own vision of a neo-classical cultural revival; D.H. Lawrence and his attacks on false gods, pornography, and industry; Wyndham Lewis' satirical exposés of fashionable political ideologies and his polemical blasts against any force which impinges on the integrity of the mind; Ransom, Tate and Blackmur, and their propaganda on behalf of their idiosyncratic kinds of poetry; the New Critics and their scrupulous specificity; George Steiner and his passionate concern for the moral relevance of art and the pressure of historical events on language; Georg Lukács and Walter Benjamin and all Marxist critiques which locate literature in a social-historical-economic grid (and, interestingly, it has been the Marxist critics who have been the most devastating opponents of Frye: see Pauline Kogan's "Northrop Frye: the High Priest of Clerical Obscurantism"); Jean-Paul Sartre and his inquiries into the psychological character and work of Baudelaire and Flaubert; Sainte-Beuve and biographical criticism; any critic who is in Baudelaire's phrase, "passionate, partial, political"; any critic who analyzes the tone, language, rhythms, and syntax of a single poem, novel, or play; any critic who examines the moral effects of literature and its relationship to questions of human relations; any critic who evaluates the quality of a writer's work; in fact, anybody who claims that an artist has *something to say.*

Which is why *The Anatomy of Criticism* has been referred to as the *autopsy* of criticism.

When you eradicate value-judgements, the moral dimension, the so-called interdisciplinary approach — politics, psychology, religion, contemporary social issues — and the location of a writer and his writings in time, then you risk eliminating what is humanly complex, unpredictable, dangerous, exalting. To teach students and critics to read without passion and urgency is to eradicate feeling and experience as ways of knowing. Bluntly stated, the study of literature cannot be a science or a pseudo-science. Literature, if it is to have an effect, cannot be reduced to a study of myths, themes, and conventions without potential harm being done to how we *apprehend.*

Frye appears to abhor the uniqueness of an individual work,

the historically located, the relationship of a writer's ideas to his public, the value of an independent mind's judgement. Donald Davie, in *Articulate Energy: An Inquiry into the Syntax of English Poetry*, calls the chapter in which he attacks Frye, "The Reek of the Human." And that title illuminates my point. It is as if Frye cannot bear the active and the temporal, the moralistic and the political, the provisional and the multiple in literature — in short, everything which bears some ghastly imprint of human "taste." There are good reasons for this: historical and psychological criticism can be specious brands of writing. What Frye constructs without these factors is *a literal abstraction*, a conservative and impersonal edifice that consigns the individuality of an author's statement, his experience, and the reader's evaluative encounter with this, to the vagaries of unclassifiable data. Where Frye postulates that literature is the flow of universal myths through the catalyst that is the artist, it is my belief that what actually occurs is an interaction, a fusion of private will and personality, of desire and formal limitations, of individual experience and under-standing (if not, as in the case of Louis-Ferdinand Céline, of sheer perversity), of unconscious associations and cultural conditioning, of environmental forces and the *Zeitgeist*. Frye detaches his system from these vectors of experience and history, although, para-doxically, his theories constitute a sort of abstract cultural historicism. He argues that all writers are involved in one grand work — "the great code" — and then flagrantly ignores the fact that writers do not always fit in; that the history of literature is not one of a gentlemanly coming to terms with external myths; that artists generally *are* aware of the reciprocity between life (reality) and the imagination. The human experience as reflected in art is, I repeat, multiple, spontaneous, paradoxical, and probably irre-ducible to suave monolinear concepts of literary form.

Because Frye ignores that complexity, the tension between the individual and the historical, tradition and the *Zeitgeist*, is omitted from his writings. And this is a considerable omission. T.S. Eliot's essay, "Tradition and the Individual Talent" — which has a signal position in Frye's philosophy — stresses two factors, not one: Tradition *and* the individual. I can only assume that Frye wilfully misreads Eliot's slippery tone and avoids that poet's subversive subordinate clauses. Frye sometimes approvingly quotes Eliot's famous statement that: "Poetry is not a turning loose of emotion, but an escape from emotion; it is not the expression of personality but an escape from personality. But, of course, only those who have personality and emotions know what it means to want to escape from these things."[13] But here Eliot is fully, even painfully, aware of personality and its role, and not even his own sophisticated attempt to deflect the reader from the poet can eliminate the imprint of the quality and integrity of his experiences.

So to judge from *The Anatomy of Criticism*, *The Educated Imagination*, *The Well-Tempered Critic*, and *The Stubborn Structure*, a poem's uniqueness should be ignored by the "true" critic and the reader, a novel's recreation of reality in order to see is irrelevant, and a work of art's insistence on the energy of change has no place in the classroom. These aspects are "ordered to be silent" for the purpose of study. You would never think that anyone who has absorbed Frye's concepts, or has been educated by his imagination, could ever conceive that in the past books have been burned, banned, and confiscated, that artists have been exiled, gagged, and jailed, that a pursuit of truth may be involved, that works of literature may have an individual subversiveness which deny their place in orderly *schemata*. As George Steiner has written: "Reading is a mode of action"; and: "To read well entails great risks"; statements in which you could replace "reading" with "writing." These are acts done in the world; they are a part of life; and that is where their moral value lies.

My charge that Frye ignores individuality and personality pertains to his disregard for the specificity of voice in a poem or novel. The voice can only be listened to on an individual basis; the critic and the reader should be alert to the beat of a particular presence. Frye seems immune to internal relations, to questions of diction, rhythm, and syntax. Compare his writings on Wallace Stevens in *Spiritus Mundi* (1976) to F.R. Leavis' close readings of Wordsworth in *Revaluations*. Frye's myth criticism works better with some writers, like T.S. Eliot or Milton, than with others. However, you do not find acute readings of Pound or William Carlos Williams, or any of the existentialist novelists like Norman Mailer. He can instruct a student to comprehend categories and principles, but I wonder whether his influence is a good one on a student's ability to see and hear, to attend to the particularities of a writer's technique, that which distinguishes an Eliot from a Pound. His schemes may sharpen your awareness of shapely systems at work in cultural history, but they cannot alert you to perceptions of specific relations. He does not give *focus*.

This avoidance of voice corresponds to Frye's penchant for monolithic systems and "theoria," and for maintaining the mask of disinterested scholarship. And these are the great cracks in his critical edifice: the urge to classify and reduce, the glorification of pseudo-scientific methods, the unacknowledged idealist prejudices, the "contemptus mundi," the neutralization of criticism. As we have seen, Frye shrugs off value-judgements and moral evaluations. Yet is this possible? Every one of Frye's critical tenets carries a value-judgement in it. Frye cannot avoid the "revelation" that he is anything but disinterested. See, for example, his bristling essay on Wyndham Lewis, "Neo-Classical Agony" (*The Hudson Review*, Volume X, Number 4, Winter 1957), which is an orgy of moral evaluations and academic distaste made in response to a writer whom Frye cannot stomach or categorize. Through every book Frye has written we find similar "slips." Now this merely shows what serious writers and critics have openly admitted for centuries: we are value-making creatures, who need art as a balance, a way of apprehending reality, as a means of understanding and focussing critical intelligence. Frye stubbornly, even perversely, avoids this, clinging to exclusive notions of knowledge and study and theory. Yet are these positions not values, too? Do they not imply moral decisions? Do they not indicate preferences? Is knowledge entirely objective? and if it were, or could be, would it be human? Complete objectivity is the stance of a god, and despite his deification by academia, Frye — as far as I know — has not yet achieved that eminent status. And while there are moments in Frye's later books when he moves toward an explicit moral declaration (the myths of freedom and concern) and an awareness of the limitations of systematic-conceptual criticism, the ramifications of his argument have not changed fundamentally since *The Anatomy of Criticism*.

What we are left with that is valuable in Frye's work is the comprehensiveness of his concepts, his subtle synthesis of ideas, and the grace and richness you find in his prose, particularly in *The Great Code* (1982). No other Canadian prose writer has had such a dream. If what he invents finally misleads, it is because of the role he assigns to the critic and the tranquilizing effect of his closed system.

There are two clear choices for the function of criticism which emerge from Frye's theoretical works. One is toward the deciphering of codes, the attainment of disinterestedness, and the freedom of the imagination in the scholar's den, "the room of one's own." The other is toward the critic in society, subject to its perilous winds, offering his disturbances and perceptions to preserve the sharp morality and progressiveness of the mind. One is ideal and exegetical; the other is practical and public.

Interestingly, it is in *Fearful Symmetry* that we find Frye making this distinction. He writes that:

>...Blake's willingness to become a public leader of art shows a confusion in his mind between two things which are carefully distinguished in the Prophecies: the imagination and the will... the struggle of art to perfect its vision and the attempt of the will to alter the world of experience. If Blake had listened to the "Rintrah" within him, he would have been told that as a public figure he would have to give the public what it wanted: an ambiguous phrase, resting on an inability to distinguish between what the public imagination wants and what the public Selfhood wants. *The only legitimate compulsion on the artist is the compulsion to clarify the form of his work, and in accepting other compulsions he is at once trapped in compromise. His forms are spoiled by the shifting of emphasis necessary for didactic purposes....* (*Fearful Symmetry*, pp. 412-413, emphasis mine)

There is of course truth in what Frye says about clarification of form. However, I believe this is a misinterpretation of what the artist's relationship to his public often is, focussing for polemical reasons on "compromise" and "didacticism." I find a curious confusion here between didactic and moral art. Didacticism is "how to": it is a way of telling you how to live. Moral art is concerned with the accurate illumination of human relationships and situations. Blake, like other writers, saw a need for the artist to be engaged in debate with a public, or else "the voice of one crying in the wilderness" (which is, after all, a revolutionary call, carrying in it a demand for radical awareness), cries to nothing, to himself, or to mere appreciators of form. Exegesis by experts is necessary, especially for poets like Blake who present a compli- cated surface. But art for itself, criticism for itself, in these troubled tragi-comic times, is a failure of nerve, a refusal to enter into debate with a confused and complacent society. I can only conclude that an education received from Frye would result in a generation of sophisticated, poetry-quoting conformists, who — resembling those lofty clerical guardians playing the glass bead game in Hermann Hesse's *Magister Ludi* — cannot use their trained intellects for anything other than the identification and discussion of "significant" patterns.

I have said that Frye's theory resembles Wilde's in "The Decay of Lying," minus several important characteristics, like a vision of reality, a true sense of satire, an awareness of the enemy. He is an academic Wilde, as it were, without "pen, pencil, and poison," hence not in the least bit *wild*. His hyperborean disdain for all things real, for a literature whose meaning is "out there," for any moral imperative, can perhaps be summed up in this statement from Wilde's essay:

> We have mistaken the common livery of the age for the vesture of the Muses, and spend our days in the sordid streets and hideous suburbs of our vile cities when we should be out on the hillside with Apollo.[14]

For Frye, reality is a construct, a feat of the imagination, that which human beings "have no business with." Thus we see him after class, ambling along Avenue Road, briefcase in hand, disappearing into his obscure inward reveries, his mind enclosed in archetypes, the timeless, the mythical. He shyly avoids the stares and stuttered "hellos" of students and vanishes into his office with his typewriter and books, leaving behind on chalkboards various diagrams and grids, a system of concepts and categories, a world without moral judgement, himself perhaps a construct now, a fiction, hardly existing, *Northrop Frye*, a catalyst for vast impersonal schemes that exist *a priori*, like one of Jorge Luis Borges' creations, a man who dreamed himself out of reality, away from the sordid streets and hideous suburbs, in his inaccessible den, with Apollo, and the other gods of his dreamland.

(1982)

McLuhan and Frye, "Either/Or"

A philosophy is the expression of a man's intimate character.
William James

"I never had a theory of media. My approach has always been perceptual and not conceptual. What I have perceived in *The Global Village* created by instantaneous information is a threat to human identity and the erasure of our way of life."[1]

Marshall McLuhan wrote those words in September, 1979, shortly before he experienced the stroke which left him, literally, speechless. The statement is one of his clearest declarations and presents the strategy and structure from within which he worked.

"I am a literary critic," Northrop Frye announces on the first page of *Creation and Recreation* (1980), "mainly concerned with English literature, and I have recently developed a special interest in the way the Bible has affected the structure and imagery of that literature. The first word to attract one's notice in both fields is the word creation. Page one of the Bible says that God created the world; page one of the critic's handbook, not yet written, tells him that what he is studying are human creations. In this book I should like to look at certain aspects of the conception or metaphor of creation..."[2]

This quotation reveals Frye's intentions and schemes. Aside from the differences in tone and rhythm — McLuhan: urgent, sharp, immediate; Frye: slow, logical and professorial — the two passages indicate the radical divergence in their thinking.

There are of course similarities between them. Both were Canadians partially educated in England, Frye at Oxford in the 1930s, McLuhan at Cambridge at approximately the same time. Both became University of Toronto teachers. Both were conservative in their beliefs and habits. Both wrote from perspectives which were grounded in religious conviction. Both have superficially similar concerns for myth. But from then on, they represent the two separate paths that are open for writers and thinkers and teachers, an "Either/Or" which has echoes in the intellectual arena of Canada itself.

For McLuhan, the fragment, the aphorism, the probe, form the basis of his tactics. The world is in ruins and to read its runes the writer must become available to the tensions and adopt an appropriate style. McLuhan's method is centred in the spasmodic-paradoxical-polemical approaches of the non-systematic thinkers like Kierkegaard and Nietzsche. Wyndham Lewis' satirical techniques provided another primary model, and *The Gutenberg Galaxy* is in many ways Lewis' *Time and Western Man* (1927) turned on its head. McLuhan worked with "a heap of broken images" in order to allow the reader the freedom to choose his own evaluative process. He was a tester: perception comes first; conception follows later. Humour was part of his method; so was the collage.

Frye is a dialectical-conceptual thinker who approaches the literary experience through theory. The dialectician is concerned with argument, systematic analysis, and consistency, leading to theoretical architecture, a synthesis. He assumes a single point-of-view over the mosaic, or the multiple perspective, and organizes his material around a line of logic, which is his thesis. One of Frye's debts is to Hegel, as he acknowledges when he says of *The Great Code* that: "Certain preliminary questions, which I had thought would be contained within an introductory chapter or two, expanded, first into an enormous Hegelian preface, and finally into a volume in its own right."[3]

McLuhan's strategy was perceptual and rhetorical, as I have quoted him as saying. He was concerned with discovery and understanding. This is why McLuhan claimed that he did not have a theory. He had a method which stressed observation, audience reception, and aphoristic soundings, what Kierkegaard once called "indirect communication."[4] McLuhan's method was certainly conducted from a rooted position; however, there was never anything *systematic* or ideologically consistent about his approach, which is why, I believe, it is difficult to locate the precise content of his argument.

Frye's work emerged from the New Critical tradition and moved into an area currently popular in scholastic circles: the theoretical package, or Theme, derived from readings of literary "texts." In this realm the critic now has the autonomy of the creator. Frye is capable of writing elegant discursive prose: he has a gift for the paragraphic period and the well-turned phrase. Frye can also be a perceptive critic, as many of his short essays show, where he is, contrary to received opinion, often at his best. McLuhan's pages frequently read like they were randomly tossed together, like some "roll of the dice," and just happened to end up in one book. From the perspective of scholarship, Frye's books are impeccably researched and argued; McLuhan's works are full of crazed interpretations and odd lapses. For Frye a contradiction, inconsistency or a misquotation would be a disaster; but for McLuhan a contradiction could lead to controversy, which could lead to new insight.

Curiously, there *are* hints in *The Anatomy of Criticism* that indicate Frye may have had other intentions for his work. One of the most startling passages is the following on Menippean Satire, which appears after a discussion of the encyclopaedic-iconoclastic strain in Petronius and Swift:

> This creative treatment of exhaustive erudition is the organizing principle of the greatest Menippean satire in English before Swift, Burton's *Anatomy of Melancholy*. Here human society is studied in terms of the intellectual pattern provided by the conception of melancholy, a symposium of books replaces dialogue, and the result is the most comprehensive survey of human life in one book that English literature had seen since Chaucer... The word "anatomy" in Burton's title means a dissection or analysis, and expresses very accurately the intellectualized approach of his form. We may as well adopt it as a convenient name to replace the cumbersome and in modern times rather misleading "Menippean satire." (p. 311-312)

Sly Frye. The alert reader immediately notes that the author's study itself is called an "anatomy." With mounting excitement you begin to see the parallels with Burton's book — "exhaustive erudition," "society studied in terms of the intellectual pattern provided by... a single conception," "anatomy... means dissection or analysis"; and then in the above quotation, Frye's deadpanned suggestion that "anatomy" is a more useful critical term than "Menippean satire." Thus it may be that Frye's intentions were nothing less than to satirize the western empirical critical tradition, to establish a closed system which is unusable if you do not accept its premises, and so create a *summa* that is an end and not a means or a new beginning.

As for McLuhan, we must question if the obscurities and the apparent moral complacency in his writings can be entirely justified. Is there an aspect of his thinking which is cheap and distorting? To some extent, yes. The instant McLuhan became his message — the mass-sage — he became part of the process he hated. For when we set aside his personal morality and conservatism, the provisional and strategic nature of much of his thought, we are still left with a terrifying sense of relaxation and commercialization. This cannot be denied if we are to treat him seriously. McLuhan must be located within that which he detested. If we do not do this, then his self-contradictions could ultimately negate him. The remains will only be shattered pieces.

To sacrifice criticism for perception is a first step. Indeed, we must see. After: review and revaluation. McLuhan laid the ground for the first step and did not live long enough to fulfill the next. His criticism can be found in his books sometimes between the lines, and sometimes openly. Example: "To describe these processes is neither endorsement nor prescription. Every man feels he has a right to defend his own ignorance even when it mucks up millions of lives. My hope is to snap somnambulists out of their highly motivated and destructive trances."[5] But time did not allow McLuhan to fully enter the critical fray. So those who knew him fill in the gaps. And the rest will have to wait for the posthumous work.

Northrop Frye makes an excellent target because he is always clear, connected, and static. The nobility of his efforts rests in his attempt to re-member the structures of our imagination, to arrest the rushed modern pace and synthesize knowledge. His writings have had a greater influence in Canada than Marshall McLuhan's. Irving Layton's battle against the Frye school of poets and teachers was based on the correct assumption that the impersonality Frye advocated was antithetical to his own "ars poetica." Layton understood Frye because he is himself so *thoroughly* imbued with dialectics and ideology and myth, indeed with a remarkably consistent personal vision of the world, that it would be easy for him to see what there was to oppose. Their honourable and inevitable conflict was one of precisely opposite parts of the same dialectic. McLuhan is more mobile and ambiguous and difficult to catch. He was a man of paradox and analogy, a poet-philosopher who loved to confuse his enemies by sometimes using their own arguments and by occasionally appearing to be in favour of that which he opposed.

Nevertheless, McLuhan was a thinker who used concrete evidence, the word in the world; Frye begins with theory, the text in the void.[6] The choice between them is not just a matter of taste: it is the way through which attention to the world can be reached.

(1983)

Part Two

The Literary Ring

The arena is well demarcated from the outside world... People always feel where it is, even if they are not thinking of it. Shouts from the arena carry far and, when it is open at the top, something of the life which goes on inside communicates itself to the surrounding city... But however exciting these communications may be, an uninhibited flow into the arena is not possible....

Elias Canetti,
"The Crowd as a Ring."

I. The Forces and Figures of "Can.Lit."

Legend has it that when Portuguese explorers first sailed up the St. Lawrence River and beheld the new land, they were moved to exclaim: "*Ka-nada.*" Which can be roughly translated to mean "nothing there." There was of course something. The Indian residents would not — and did not — relish being regarded as nothing. But that stigma still haunts many Canadian writers. We hear it sneaking into their critical evaluations, making the speakers seem timid or like propagandists for government cultural committees. The uneasiness lingers: how can a place of silence and strangers, of empty spaces and ferocious weather, of conservative culture and cautious politics, become something, indeed anything, at all.

Today there is much talk in Canadian writing about literature and tradition. Twenty-five years ago it was the fashion to complain that there was no genuine poetry, fiction, and criticism. Now the tide has turned and the opposite sentiments are expressed. We have a literature. We have arrived. Our culture flourishes. Thus to counteract this sense of "nothing," Canadian writing became "CanLit" and "Can.Cult." at some point in the 1970s. If this is vague, it is because I cannot precisely determine when the event took place. But once it did, there was at last a category, an identifiable *thing* which could be ranked beside Am.Lit., Brit.Lit., Germ.Lit., It.Lit., Nor.Lit., etcetera, and judged accordingly. Actually, I could set the official recognition date as 1974: the year Canadian literature was incorporated as a business, when CANLIT, a nonprofit organization, was established at the Glendon College campus of York University to provide research on Canadian writing, publishing, and culture.

It was, however, in the late 1960s and early '70s that the "renaissance" whirl was truly launched. Voices were raised; publicity began; prophecies were made. Writers were sought for Writers-in-Residence programs at Universities; credit courses were introduced; teachers were hired and given CANLIT books *Course Countdown: A Quantitative Study of Canadian Literature in the Nation's Secondary Schools*, *Something for Nothing: An Experimental Book Exposure Programme*, and *CanLit Teacher's Crash Course Kit*; magazines with titles like *Delta*, *Descant*, and *Exile* flourished; new names were heralded, like Hodgins, Ondaatje and Musgrave; trade magazines like *Books in Canada* and *Quill and Quire* enlarged in importance and circulation; small publishers expanded, like Talonbooks (British Columbia), NeWest (Alberta), Oberon, Coach House, Anansi (Ontario), Fiddlehead (New Brunswick); the Writers' Union, the union des ecrivains quebecois, and the League of Canadian Poets were formed; the Canada Council increased its budget from less than a million dollars in the early 70s to over 7 million in the early 80s; institutional support grew in influence from the CBC (radio especially, with shows like "Anthology"), to the separate Provincial Arts Councils; buttons appeared with messages like "PSST! Wanna Read a Canadian Book" (produced by McClelland and Stewart, the *Canadian* publishers, in 1972) and "Read/dammit" (Canadian Book Information Centre, in 1976, with a maple leaf in the middle of the "d"); PaperJacks and Seal paperback originals were founded; editors, like Robert Fulford (*Saturday Night*), Anna Porter (formerly at Seal), Jack McClelland and Peter Newman (*Maclean's*), became media stars (all of whom, incidentally, are friends); fashion magazines displayed photographs of the latest badly-dressed literary icon; aging men-of-letters were asked for fresh pronouncements; agents started selling and guiding raw provincial talent ("If your story is about Goldilocks and the three little bears, then bring on the bears," goes one well-known piece of agent's advice); articles were published — and are still published — with titles like "The Renaissance of Can.Lit.," "How Can.Lit. is viewed abroad," "CanLit Rising," "What Can.Lit. has to say," "Can.Lit. comes of age"; and awards — awards *galore*, The Governor General's Award, the Seal Books $50,000 First Novel Award ($10,000 prize, plus $40,000 non-returnable advance on royalties), the Books in Canada First Novel Award, the Gerald Lampert and Pat Lowther Memorial Awards for poetry, to name a few out of dozens.

When the 1980s began, the situation had again changed. The

pace slackened; a new gloom was cast. Book publishers were taken over by conglomerates, following a trend that had been happening for several decades in the United States; some went bankrupt or into receivership; production costs skyrocketed; and weary, over-worked editors of major publishing houses started confessing, "I don't know how to read any more," as they searched for the best-seller which would keep their house afloat in wavering economic times.

Thus the "Can.Lit." industry was formed, and like any market it has its corporations, coteries, captains, Public Relations men, assassins, and slaves. These are the service organizations and cliques who run things. It has been claimed by some that there are no cabals in "Can.Lit." To any political thinker that is of course nonsense. "Family Compacts" always direct the forces of culture. Yet you will hear literati in the "Can.Lit." echelons declaring that there are no prejudices or backroom powers determining reputations, subverting others, usually with attacks on the disreputable character of the author, and perpetuating particular attitudes. However, you can assume that if this is being officially denied, it is true.

Clearly, "a charmed few" control the movements of "Can.Lit." I call this "the fertilizer."[1] There are the Media groups, with Robert Fulford, Peter Newman, Jack McClelland, Pierre Berton, Robert Weaver; the Writers' Union, formed in the early 1970s by Graeme Gibson, Margaret Atwood, Marian Engel and others; and the superstars, like Atwood and Frye (the Victoria College Group).[2] The making and breaking of reputations occurs courtesy of the reviewers of *The Globe and Mail*, *The Toronto Star*, *Saturday Night*, *Maclean's*, the CBC (radio and TV), and the better known literary magazines like *The Canadian Forum* and *Quill and Quire*. Word of mouth is always helpful in what is, after all, a small, even intimate scene, though recognition in the major American dailies and journals will shore up a rising Name. Readers determine interest through sales, and *The Stone Angel* and *The Apprenticeship of Duddy Kravitz* have proved to be enduring sellers. The big Canadian best-sellers still tend to be "non-books" like hockey books, garden books, and consumer service books.[3] However, in Canada, the preservers and perpetuators of Name remain in the universities. The universities provide a livelihood and audience, the mechanics of reputation, an extensive involve-ment which you can evaluate for yourself when I report on its impact.

You may have observed that the majority of the arbiters of

Name and Taste are located in Toronto. The inference is that Toronto is the seat of literary reputation. Despite centres of activity in Montreal, Edmonton, and Vancouver, this is a safe assumption. (Fascinating fact: *The Canadian Forum, This Magazine*, the Association of Canadian Publishers, the Canadian Book Information Centre, the Literary Press Group, *Canadian Business Magazine*, Key Porter Books, *Quill and Quire*, and *Toronto Life*, share offices in the same Toronto building which houses the most notoriously frantic singles' bars in the city.) The major publishers are in Toronto, like McClelland and Stewart and Macmillan, who between them have a corral of writers, from Atwood, Laurence, Layton, Richler, and Farley Mowat, to Davies, Gallant, and W.O. Mitchell. There is also Lester and Orpen Dennys, General Publishing and Seal Books. So, as it was once said of New York City, make it in Toronto and you have made it in the nation.

However, the Toronto arbiters of Name and Taste do not have the power of *The New York Review of Books, The New Yorker, Time Magazine*, or *The New York Times Review of Books*. William French is not Arthur Mizener; Robert Fulford is not Granville Hicks. You do get incestuous reviewing by "familiars" — those acquaintances within the literary or service groups; Timothy Findley on Marian Engel, for example, and vice versa, in the Book and Letters-to-the-Editor pages of *The Toronto Star* and *The Globe and Mail*. The "Can.Lit." literary establishment confers mythic status *post facto*, and often grudgingly, as when a writer like Richler has already achieved a considerable amount of success, or when exile Mavis Gallant wins the Governor General's Award. Recall the flurry of interest by the public and the media in 1982 when Irving Layton was nominated for the Nobel Prize by the Italians and South Koreans. To no one's surprise, the appearance of a new stellar Name, the overnight sensation, is rare amongst these prudent and cool forces and figures.

The other important influences on "Can.Lit." are government institutions. The CBC produces radio-plays, discussion programs, interview shows, and occasional documentaries for television. Many writers use it as a financial refuge, writing scripts and working on programs of various kinds. Short-stories, poems, and plays are frequently produced and presented on CBC radio. The "Ideas" show (FM) serves as a vehicle for scholars and independents, and "Morningside" (AM) allows writers the chance to be interviewed and aired nationally.

The Canada Council, though, is *the* financial force in Canada. It has affected everyone from publishers and printers to poets and professors. I can speak from personal experience as I have (I confess) received several grants over the last few years. I know of no novelist, poet or essayist, no university or writer's program, who has not had support from the omnipresent Council or its provincial counterparts. Glance at the acknowledgement page of almost any Canadian book published since 1974 and the debt will be verified. Even the Writers' Union is largely funded by them. However, the range of the Council's work is too vast and intricate for a brief analysis here. That is a project which should be undertaken on a large scale, an endeavour which I am sure will be undertaken soon, and which will, assuredly, be funded by the great Council itself.

Nevertheless, certain details are worth pointing out. The granting of awards is sometimes governed by confusing principles; they are often given to writers, publishers and organizations for inexplicable reasons. Political patronage, influence, regional representation, changing governments, publishers' requests, letters of recommendation from established authors who may themselves be involved in the Council's selection committees — all these can play a part in a decision. Unfortunately, it has been the mistakes the Council has made which have led to outcries about socialism, state control, subsidization of mediocrity, pampered poets, and art which cannot stand the test of the marketplace. There is always waste in such an extensive program; but without the Council's aid, what we call culture in the Dominion would be a floundering joke. The Council has played the part of an impersonal patron, like the aristocrats of a renaissance city state. Their work is the kind of government activity that Ezra Pound, Wyndham Lewis, and T.S. Eliot agitated for. Also, with incomes of most Canadian authors existing below the poverty-line, the Council has *saved* more often than it has *savaged.* Finally, to my knowledge, the policy of the Council has always been one of "hands-off." Once a grant is given, there is no interference from bureaucrats. The artist is free to work; the responsibility is thereafter his. And that is an important distinction between the impact of the Canada Council and other institutions, like the University.

Of course the whole question of money and power in the reputation-building centres may seem to outsiders like a trivial and laughable matter. I assure you that it is not. Few writers are self-supporting, and so many are dependent on the benevolent Council, on journalism, the CBC, and kind relatives and friends, that it is impossible to laugh all the way to the bank. Instead, you grin and bear the lack of a public, and go to the government, cap in hand, asking: please sir, may I have some more? Money makes scenes.

Big publishers are interested in the bottom-line — will it sell? — and turn to what non-readers demand. Small publishers fill the gap, though without distribution their books seep into view slowly.

To publish is to go public. ("Publish": from the Latin "publicare", to make public.) What you can gather from these observations is that a literary community is always structured around clubs, like the Bloomsbury group in London during the 1920s. Thus the intellectual atmosphere can become one of "intense localization," to borrow an ugly phrase from the sociologists. Unquestionably, though, the University remains the greatest stabilizing and localizing force in "Can. Lit.," and we turn to it now as part of our tour around the literary ring.

II. The University as Hidden Ground

It is commonly acknowledged that much of Canadian literature is dominated by academics and authors with positions as professors and lecturers at universities. Our two most widely respected intellectuals, Northrop Frye and the late Marshall McLuhan, have been, of course, prominent members of the University community. Other authors and poets teach at major institutions, such as Hugh MacLennan, Robertson Davies, Rudy Wiebe, Tom Marshall, Robert Kroetsch, Hugh Hood, Barry Callaghan, Eli Mandel, Frank Davey, Roch Carrier, Jay Macpherson, James Reaney, Clark Blaise, Dennis Duffy, D.G. Jones, Michael Ondaatje, Aritha Van Herk, Ian McLachlan, George Grant, F.R. Scott, Dorothy Livesay, Louis Dudek, Robin Skelton, Josef Skvorecky, and Miriam Waddington. Many more, such as Dennis Lee, Jack Hodgins, David Helwig, Peter Such, W.P. Kinsella, Matt Cohen, George Bowering, Earle Birney, Douglas LePan, John Metcalf, George Woodcock, and Marian Engel, have spent time at universities, or are otherwise affiliated as chancellors, visiting lecturers, and writers-in-residence, like Margaret Atwood, Leo Simpson and W.O. Mitchell. Indeed, the Writer-in-Residence Syndrome is a virtual epidemic in "Can.Lit." (John Metcalf's *General Ludd* is a satire on this.) Even mavericks like Irving Layton, Earle Birney, and Mordecai Richler have taught creative writing courses and programs in modern fiction and poetry. That this fact has remained largely unexamined is a fascinating aspect of Canadian literary studies. For the issue is more important than it might at first appear: if we are in the midst of a literary renaissance, where are many of the major figures located? out of what *milieu* are they writing? what does this indicate about shifts in literary centres? what is the kind of literature often produced by these authors and poets? and who is the writing *for?*

The location is easy enough to identify: in academia: in the classrooms, offices and committees of an educational institution which is by its nature conservative and often conformist, withdrawn from most of society's explosive changes, and self-referential (cloistered). The literary universe becomes the University.[1] The effect of this "ground" on writers and poets is also easy to identify: only a few have discovered the explosive nature of modernist literature. (But then neither have most of the publishers or the audience.) With the exception of McLuhan's work, Layton's poetry, Richler's novels, and certain younger writers trying to modernize themselves, there are few poets, novelists and critics independently challenging, observing, questioning, evaluating our past, present, and future, our culture, habits and institutions, the experience of reality as if it were right there in front of them. If, as Wyndham Lewis felt, the artist is dedicated to the "radical exposure" of (to) "the brick-making of the New Jerusalem," then many of these University authors have contented themselves with being sequestered in the sanctums and silent studies of English Literature programs and writing classes, whose objective it is to *study others.* A soul-shattering modernism cannot happen when artists are contemplating it from a safe distance.

There are good economic reasons for the retreat into academia. Given the small audience in Canada, the supposed decline of literacy, the impact of the electronic media, the lack of a literary community outside the University, you may ask what a writer is to do. If a responsive audience is not present, then the artist must look for other means of support. But we should not delude ourselves into thinking that this flight does not have a cost. With a few notable exceptions, the University poets and authors, writers-in-residence and creative composition teachers have created a literature of narcissistic self-contemplation and mandarin staleness, of conventionality and acceptance.

That the University has assumed this dominant position in Canadian writing is nearly an unprecedented situation in Western literary history. Not since the medieval age has one institution been so *pervasively* involved in the creation and support of artists. (The Oxford Movement during the Pre-Raphaelite period would perhaps be an exception.) The post-World War II scene in Canada runs counter to the early developments of the twentieth century.

In no country were the giants supported by academia. Can you imagine D.H. Lawrence, Pound, Proust, Joyce, Wyndham Lewis, Hemingway, Fitzgerald, Mann, William Carlos Williams, Eugene O'Neill, Sinclair Lewis, and Thomas Wolfe, indeed any of the artists responsible for what we call modernism, teaching regularly at a University? This is not to say they were not educated, often erudite men. The encyclopedic accomplishments of Pound and Joyce are known. T.S. Eliot took his degree from Harvard, and even Thomas Wolfe, in some ways the wildest of them all, was a Harvard man. But though they may have spent time in academia, these writers did not stay on the campus. They struck out into the turbulent world of their times, and wrote of what they saw, heard, knew, felt. The tendency now is to look on this period as a "Golden Age," and though it would be simplistic to attribute the modern crises of art (crises of subject; crises of form; crises of audience) to the dominance of the University, it would be equally simplistic to deny its impact.

The presence of the University in Canadian literature has several major effects, and one could extrapolate this to include the American scene, with John Barth serving as prime example. The first is, as I have said, the University as ground: it is the hidden environment, the financial support, with its cultural assumptions, rules, and procedures. Second, the University is looked to as the arbiter of critical values and judgements. Many of the University writers write books for the teachers they know will read them and then teach them in English or Comparative Literature programs. Lastly, and most damaging, the University becomes the final audience for the work of art. This has resulted in what I call "literary narcissism," or twentieth-century Scholasticism. The artist as teacher becomes an academic-critic, and the critic reverently reads other academic-critics, and begins to study criticism itself as if *it* were the primary object of attention. The result has been, as the poet John Crowe Ransom prophetically announced in 1939 — and in a fashion he did not mean or foresee — "the Age of Criticism." Again, this is not just a Canadian problem. There is a sense in which the post-war proliferation of Structuralists, Semioticians, Formalists, and Grammatologists is one aspect of the academic as audience for art. These critics are often serious and dedicated people, but as Malcolm Cowley writes in "The New Age of Rhetoricians," which describes this state in American universities, the condition they have created in "Can.Lit." resembles that of the Ming Dynasty and the Roman Empire under the Antonines.[2]

A time which is "An age of Criticism (of Criticism)" or, better yet, "an Age of Specialists," is probably not a major creative period. There are exceptions in Canada, the United States, Europe, and South America, although the only contemporary artists who have remained in academia and produced consistently fine work are Saul Bellow, Guy Davenport, and the late John Gardner. Bellow's novel *The Dean's December* serves as a model for the image of the artist as disillusioned academic in an exclusive world that has divorced itself from feeling and the circus of the present. But when the scholars become the *main* audience for poetry, fiction, and the serious essay (and I am thinking of the essays of George Steiner, Michael Hamburger, F.R. Leavis, and Irving Howe), art becomes "Egyptianized," a mummy, fit only for immaculate display in a museum. It no longer has an active function in society; it becomes an object of contemplation and structural mechanics, a battleground for "Theory" and private games. Without a public, literature echoes in a void.

The issue resolves into one question: what is writing supposed to do? All serious writing is based on a criticism of spiritual and intellectual values, of the quality and direction of life, and the emotional relations of people to each other and their society. Writing today is to preserve what is worthwhile, to revive, report, and reveal, and to use words and create a style. Literary freedom requires a command of time. When the writer is protected by a University, he speaks only to himself, to the already converted, or out of a milieu that is a part of the structure he may wish to criticize. The artist is thus too rigidly "placed." Indeed, it is almost impossible to imagine a Professor of Literature becoming one of the country's most important rebels. (Think of Baudelaire or Sean O'Casey in that context.) This situation has virtually deprived us of the urgency of great art, for art must break this mold if it is to *mean* — and mean beyond the self-referential atmosphere of systems and curricula, blackboards and chalk.

An image: The writer in his office at a major Canadian University. All day students have trooped dutifully in and out to discuss grades and papers. The room is bright, airy, booklined. There are few clothing rules (not at this school) so the poet-novelist wears denim. He smokes a pipe. His hair is long at the sides; he is going bald at the top. There are meetings to chair: tenure and fees committees; scholarships to evaluate. He has his own articles to write, and colleagues to meet, those scholars of Comparative Literature and the Age of Dryden, Pope and Swift. The writer now thinks in footnotes. Every day the conversation at lunch, or tea, or in the faculty lounge in the evening, consists of civilized one-upmanship. Every day there are polished turns of phrase, the students, the struggle to keep up with what's new in Semiotics, textual analysis, the latest defence of New Critical methods (a bias *he* shares) and neurological discoveries (right and left hemisphere discussions now appearing everywhere). The professor, however, is different. He is an author, a poet. His books are even on a Canadian literature course held at this University! Naturally, he is treated differently. He is "a bit of an eccentric," a potential man of action, after all ... *a writer*. But he knows he has to teach a course in the afternoon on the European novel in translation. In the morning, a course on modern poetry; later in the week, a seminar on D.H. Lawrence. Even if the muse called, writing would have to wait until the summer. Then he could do his real work. In the meantime, back to the hobnobbing with those annotators, interpreters, exegetes, and experts on Quattrocento love sonnets, back to the world of secondary sources.

* * *

Do not misunderstand me: this is no hostility to the classoom and the campus. I am a product of that world, too. The University has, as well, supported writers of notorious difficulty, like Ezra Pound, and those who threatened to fade into obscurity, like Hermann Broch. It has also produced great teachers, like F.R. Leavis and Marshall McLuhan. But the rise of the University as a literary sanctum-sanctuary since the 1940s is without parallel. No place is ideal. To read and write well, and the vitality of language and critical intelligence, are the aims. The problem is with polarization and specialization, with the widening gap between the University's universe and the public one. On one side, we have intellectual retrenchment, and on the other, creeping dumbness, zap, speed, and flash. Audiences have been lost and the role of the writer has been diminished. Where *is* the independent artist and intellectual to stand? Saul Bellow has said: "Critics and professors have declared themselves the true heirs and successors of the modern classic authors."[3] This would be catastrophic if it were true; but if the writer has any responsibility to his public and to his time, it is surely to provoke understanding, to reach readers and to retrieve language.

So far Canada has existed in the frontier zone of modernism. The last twenty-five years in "Can.Lit." are often referred to as the "Classical Period," for after comes the deluge, the delusion, or the beginnings of a durable canon of writing. Canadians often still pride themselves on considering their land as a "tabula rasa" (which is curious, because our cultural situation resembles a condition of interphase, a loose mosaic of differing traditions). To live in the cultural tradition of the British and the Europeans allows a certain automatic assimilation, an understanding of what there is to deal with. To be born into a "tabula rasa" means the artist must create his own stage and choose his inheritance.

We are the apprentices of this "motion." Where it is moving, where we are going, is difficult to know, although writers like George Woodcock make optimistic noises about growth and maturity. Vibrations may be felt across the Dominion, but you must first answer for yourself: who, or what, do all these writers *serve?*

(1981)

A Climate Charged:
The Intellectual Atmosphere in Canada

Life is, in itself and forever, shipwreck. To be shipwrecked is not to drown.
The poor human being, feeling himself sinking into the abyss, moves his arms
to keep afloat. This movement of the arms which is his reaction against his
own destruction, is culture — a swimming stroke. — When culture is no more
than this it fulfills its function and the human being rises above his own abyss.
But ten centuries of cultural continuity brings with it — among many
advantages — the great disadvantage that man believes himself safe, loses the
feeling of shipwreck, and his culture proceeds to burden itself with parasitic and
lymphatic matter. Some discontinuity must therefore intervene, in order that man
may renew his feeling of peril, the substance of his life. All his life-saving
equipment must fail, he must find nothing to cling to. Then his arms will once
again move redeemingly.

Ortega Y Gasset

There's no geist like the Zeitgeist.

Robert Hughes

To read the climate of writing and thinking in a literary culture is
like trying to forecast the weather: hazardous and open to
misinterpretation of the signs. The good weatherman, like the
good critic, should know more than how the wind blows: he should
be able to decipher the influxes and eddies, the unseen influences
and the off-shore turbulence. For a cultural climate can move its
contemporaries in overt and (some say) insidious ways. Sometimes
the effects are hardly recognizable; sometimes they are unavoid-
ably immediate; but there is "a spirit of the age," as the cliché goes,
which has its own possessive winds.

For over two decades the Canadian literary scene has been charged with a distinct emphasis: self-definition. Not self-knowledge, but "identity." "Who are you?" "what are we?" are the questions you often hear repeated as if in some public psychoanalytic debate. Canadian critics have been preoccupied with efforts to define, categorize, create structures and themes into which works of art could be appropriated and appreciated. There were political-social reasons for this activity: Canadians felt insecure and isolated, particularly because of their proximity to the American literary machine, and so felt the need to express a difference. Unwittingly, this insecurity has perhaps been a reflection of a larger malaise, which we would call "the death of art" syndrome. If the great heresy of the nineteenth century was the death of God, as Nietzsche and Dostoyevsky recognized, then the heresy of the twentieth century has been the declaration that "poetry is impossible" and "the novel is finished." The surrealists outrageously claimed that nothing could be accomplished in art until the complete works of Shakespeare were burned. For many, Shakespeare *has* been erased from our minds and the "art is dead" debate is a banality. But it is hard to smother the human spirit and wherever there are individuals, there is art. Fine poems, novels, stories, plays, and essays continue to be written, defying the prophecies of the gloom-pourers.[1]

Still, you cannot avoid the tremors of the global climate: it has to be faced that what was once called "High Cult" has decayed and what is considered serious has been confined to the new cloisters of the University. There the poem and the novel are reconstructed and deconstructed as a model or paradigm of interlocking graphs and charts and abstracted symbols. The novel and the poem cease to exist: they become Structures instead. The impact on Canadian writers has been less blatant than elsewhere, but because of electric atmospheric pressures writers have been forced to deal with nineteenth century nationalism or have leapt "ahead" to what has been dubbed post-modernism or "fabulism." And, as Louis Dudek has shrewdly observed: "Modernism is something that is still developing in Canada."[2] Thus the cultural mood in the country is a combination of the reactionary and the fashionable. Robertson Davies and Margaret Atwood stand at opposite extremes. One is the High Tory lecturing the age about God, Queen, and Country; the other is the author of nihilistic-romances. The mind is with the Victorians; but the milieu is "absolutely modern." In between there are poets, novelists, and essayists searching for a public and appropriate words. This has yet to be fully understood, and to do so, certain representative "Can.Lit." Guide books should be examined for traces of the yearning to define a self, place, and time.

Some quick generalities: there are factors that go into the making of a critical approach which are common to any period and should not be understood as being unique. Nevertheless, elements to be alert to are: the school or movement that the critic belongs to; the recurring phrases or concepts of the argument; the literary manner used, language being the ground to the argument. In the Canadian case, the nationalists have dominated the field and their approach is thematic, historical, political, geographical, or sociological. The nationalists have several sub-groups, the most prominent being the regionalists and the loyalists. These are political groups, whose spiritual leader is (indirectly) George Grant. An example of a University study of loyalism is Dennis Duffy's *Gardens, Covenants, Exiles* (1982); an example of a regional book is *The Rock Observed: Studies in the Literature of Newfoundland* (1979), by Patrick O'Flaherty. These books are the products of an increasing self-consciousness about what it means to be a Canadian writer, although perhaps *the* extreme example of a political-polemical literary critique is Robin Mathews' *Canadian Literature: Surrender or Revolution* (1978), a series of high-pitched essays written in response to the nationalist call of his time.[3]

Now, I recognize that "the criticism of criticism" is an unattractive result of the current revival of Dark Ages Scholasticism. You enter that arena reluctantly. But if we by-pass the scholars and daily reviewers, we can concentrate on those who are responsible for the time's stamp: the cultural theorists and thematic critics. This distinction between scholar, reviewer, and critic is important: the reviewer shapes public response through newspapers and magazines; the scholar studies literature as an object of knowledge; and the good critic remains "the practitioner," a novelist or poet himself. All true modernist writing is animated by a critical spirit. Thus Mordecai Richler, Robertson Davies, Margaret Atwood, Irving Layton, Dennis Lee, and Eli Mandel practice the trade. Of these, only Atwood, Mandel and Lee have produced full-scale non-fiction studies, while Richler, Davies and Layton have contented themselves with journalistic squibs which have been collected in *Shovelling Trouble* (1972), *The Well-Tempered Critic* (1981), and *Engagements* (1972). Richler is an entertainingly acerbic literary journalist, and Layton relies on his authorial-authoritative presence to carry through with fast, furious and frequently funny invective and satire. Their comments are often tough and turbulent, especially in the letters Layton springs on newspapers. Robertson Davies is different, though. The former Master of Massey College is urbane and refined, and in *One Half of Robertson Davies* (1977) he is *ironic*, although his critical writing is often loaded with a querulous eccentricity and dandyism.

Ideally, the public critical essay can supply a strategy for combatting dogmatism, dullness, and assorted plastic gods. But criticism today has undergone a fascinating transformation. Tom Wolfe's irreverent idea in *The Painted Word* (1975) was that you could no longer see a painting without a theory. The same has occurred in the literary enterprise. To remain supple and open and non-dogmatic has fallen into disrepute. Receptivity and intelligence and the passionate reading of experience are not enough. You must now have an arsenal of concepts, a Theory, and preferably a Continental European one. This suggests that the Literary-Theorist does not have a subordinate role: he is now in fact vastly superior to "the naive artist." In order to compete, the writer theorizes and invents a jargon. Such an attempt to be modish is Robert Kroetsch's *Labyrinths of Voice* (1982). Kroetsch's *The Studhorse Man* is surely an admirable novel, but in this book he spins out in a dialogue with two interviewers the most opaque "Game" jargon you can find outside Jacques Derrida and any devoted annotator of the later Nabokov. Example:

> We take self back into that intertextuality that you're talking about, because the self's just a kind of fragment, a shifting pattern, you see, and the notion that the self was somehow a nut somewhere that hadn't been cracked or whatever is absurd to us now. (p. 7)

For my purposes Margaret Atwood's *Survival* (1972) remains the most controversial example of the nationalist theme book. It has a thesis which acts as a grab-bag into which you stuff various specimens. "This is a book of patterns," she says (p. 11). The study is in the Northrop Frye non-evaluative, a-historical, non-biographical, structural analysis vein, where the theme is actually a series of patterns discovered to be coherently lurking deep in the textures of miscellaneous works. This can be exciting, as the theme book often becomes an ambitious cultural exposé. *Survival*'s intention is to describe "something that would make Canadian literature, as *Canadian literature*... accessible to people other than scholars and specialists...." (p. 13).

Despite *Survival*'s slap-dash approach, and the fey reticence Atwood indulges in, she is saying something important. Her theme is that the content of Canadian writing is frequently, if not entirely, survival of the victim, the isolated figure at odds with nature, society, the past, or himself. "The central symbol for Canada is... Survival... it is a multi-faceted and adaptable idea... But the main idea is... hanging on, staying alive" (pp. 32-33). The Canadian author writes out of his experience as "a failure," a loser who is crushed by implacable forces (like "Nature the Monster"). Atwood's thesis is self-effacing and morose, when you think about it. "Canadians," she writes, "show a marked preference for the negative." (p. 15) However, Atwood has indeed identified a repressed and repressive strain in Canadian writing, and she sometimes nicely describes the tensions and barren indifference with which the early authors had to contend. She does it in a breezy way with a style that is coyly mannered. But the reader should never forget that *Survival* was written at a time of nationalist fervour. It is a literary-political polemic and personal manifesto that finds its centre in Northrop Frye's explanation of "the garrison mentality" in *The Bush Garden* (1971) and Existentialist literature — notably in the idea of victimization.

Survival is weak in places. It lumps poets and novelists together indiscriminately in a thematic structure which is intolerant of nuance and difference. There is no tracing of the communication studies of Harold Innis and Marshall McLuhan, surely an indispensible factor in a nation of silence and strangers. The book has a peculiar tendency to treat minors like Ernest Buckler with excessive reverence. It is also a hastily written Guidebook for high-school and university students (without footnotes). Atwood misinterprets Margaret Laurence's stoicism, and her theme of the victim does not allow her to accurately deal with either Robertson Davies or Irving Layton. There is little serious treatment of the urban experience, which is customary amongst "Can.Lit." theorists, nor of the unusual situation of poet-novelists dominating Canadian writing, of which Ms. Atwood herself is a successful example. The book shrugs off the experience of authors from the Soviet Union, Eastern Europe, and South America, who have more to "survive" than Canadians . However, *Survival* does not aspire to thoroughness. It is a readable, though not closely reasoned, argument. It is set up as a "Survival Package" ("How to Use This Book," the Introduction says) and proceeds to show what works "fit" in "Basic Victim Positions" and are thus relevant to the cause of the newly established "Can.Lit."

Atwood has taken her share of critical barbs for the schematic generalizations and the sarcastic tone of her book. I do not think this is useful because, aside from being too easy to do, *Survival* is a provocative pioneer essay which demonstrated that there was *something* (out there) for young Canadian writers to grapple with.

Dennis Lee's *Savage Fields: An Essay in Literature and Cosmology* (1977) is a dense literary-philosophical inquiry where, in veiled terms, Heidegger and Nietzsche collide on the pages like metaphysical mastodons. But since *Savage Fields* follows in what is supposed to be the Canadian line of Exile-Isolation-Alienation-Survival, it is worth interrogating. "Savage fields" is an umbrella phrase, part abstract concept, part poetic metaphor, used to describe the vision of order and disorder on our planet. Lee has been reading Heidegger's *Being and Time* and *Poetry, Language, Thought* (or perhaps only *Poetry, Language, Thought*), because early on we are treated to non-capitalized personifications like "world" and "earth." At first, what he calls his "conceptual language" is leaden and convoluted. This is odd, because Lee's children's verse has the opposite qualities. *Alligator Pie* is not the work of someone who cannot write. Yet Lee is trying to be bold and perhaps innovative in the introduction. He is trying to do for Canadian writing what the German Romantic-Nationalists tried to do in the nineteenth century for their literature. Give it a name, an identity: "New wine in new bottles," he writes (p. 4). However, in *Savage Fields* Lee apparently wants to conceal rather than reveal. Still, obscurity is one form of engagement, and since Lee is a recognized poet, we trudge on.

The "Introduction" struggles toward epigram and pith, like Nietzsche, while trying to preserve a broad conceptual outline, like Hegel. A non-systematic method for what is in fact a systematic matter. Strange words shoot up, like "extensible" and "globalizing," in opaque phrases like "Earth appears to world as the ensemble of beings which are conscious instinct" (p. 4); and: "World has engirdled the planet; self-contradictory though it sounds, earth is increasingly world. In principle, the planet is not both wholly world and wholly earth" (p. 7); and: "Planet is seamless with itself" (p. 9). Soon into the "Introduction" and later in "Part One," we see a fog creeping in. Heideggerisms abound: *"earth assault," "world assault," "earth-in-world,"* and *"stasis, union,"* and the *"skeletal moment"* (p. 15). However, the argument seems to consist of a rather conventional "nature-civilization" conflict (or "earth-world," in Lee's terms) and so you ask: is the style supposed to be a parody?

Lee is a poet: he would not, or should not, use words carelessly. Style is argument. Lee's thick manner, then, appears to be a deliberate rhetorical device, carefully (even painfully) developed to draw your attention to "new" ideas. Either that or Lee has assimilated so much Heidegger that his English is beginning to sound as if it has been translated from German by a professor of European Existentialist Literature. Yet there is something Lee is struggling to get at, so I flipped back to the book's beginning and soldiered trustingly past the awkward compounds — "instinctually-driven planet," "consciousness-dominated planet," "earth-allies" — through the conceptualization of "the strife" between "earth" and "world" which creates "savage fields" (p. 11), and on to the analyses of Michael Ondaatje and Leonard Cohen. Lee's conceptual model is set up and two literary works are explicated to advance his argument.

Eventually the book's explicit moral surfaces in "The Problem of Savage Fields." Lee states that "Savage fields" expresses modernity (p. 41). Then in a throwaway remark, he says: "Though I loathe modernity (while being a product of it)...." At last we spot the influence of George Grant and that Conservative-Loyalist dislike of modernist culture (read: American). There are things to abhor and attack in the modern world; but we must know clearly what is dangerous before we turn away in revulsion. Paradoxically, Lee has also shown through this thin book that he is an exemplary modernist, or (if you must) *post*-modernist. You could imagine Professor John Barth applauding the conceptual seriousness, the linguistic plays, the fragmented form, the suppressed logical links, the dependence on abstract philosophy. More Heideggerisms follow: "By imagining the strife of world and earth so convincingly, as the amoral matrix of all other order, and by perceiving the impulse to dominate earth as ingrained and imperative in the very cast of men's consciousness, *Billy the Kid* achieves a marvellous portrait of world" (p. 44).

In the "Interlude," Lee generalizes about what he calls "the liberal cosmology" (p. 50). This stopped me cold. What in the world (lower case) is that? I asked. Lee wrestles for a while with a definition of liberalism, but there are gaps in the argument and the research that cause confusion. Does he identify liberalism with technology? the spirit of revolution? the urban landscape? sex? relativity? Freud? moral laziness? Does he mean... modernization? Leaps of faith are made from existential springboards into dark waters to form what look suspiciously like reactionary waves against secular modernism. I began to wonder:

is Lee a closet mystic, decrying the profane and groundless world?

The problem is that *Savage Fields* is a work for initiates familiar with the assumptions. It is helpful to have read George Grant's *Lament for a Nation* and *Technology and Empire*, Jacques Ellul, and the German authority figures that Lee is playing against. Lee's book could be considered a set of discontinuous notes on a larger yet unwritten text. McLuhan, like Nietzsche, used this approach; but he provided a lucid context with which to work. McLuhan's puns, allusions, aphorisms and subversions of the reader's expectations are part of a strategy to force you into pondering the page. This may be what Dennis Lee had in mind, and to give him his due, he admits that "It is too early to tell whether these lines of approach would be adequate for full-fledged thinking" (p. 59). We may have to wait for clarification in further volumes. *Savage Fields* is better when it shifts to practical criticism. The examination of Cohen's *Beautiful Losers* is specific, as the last pages turn unexpectedly clear, even useful, when Lee's Puritan didacticism allows him to deal with what is, albeit, a rather easy target.

Nevertheless, *Savage Fields* shows Lee deserting what he should be excelling at: language and perception. In the "Epilogue" he concludes with thoughts: "Tasks for thinking.... Cherish the gaps, holes, leaks, fissures, shortfalls, failures in world's juggernaut ascendancy. Think the coherence, non-smarmily, of world's inability to achieve what it wants.... Another go: think the partial incoherence of world's project, coherently. Describe it more radically than it cares to itself" (p. 110).

If the world (lower case) is seized by "savage fields," and some contemporary art reflects this, do we need more unreadable books? It is difficult for anyone of our generation to think or write. We are in a real sense losing our minds. *For when we lose words, we begin to lose our minds.*

I refer the reader to Elias Canetti's *Crowds and Power* (English translation: 1962), because this book is a poetic-perceptive analysis of the extensions and roots of power and masses, and the relationship between the individual and the crowd. Here a conceptual network of new terms is not introduced. Canetti explores power and coercion, with a pessimistic precision: he makes us see and think. No neat schemes are deposited like Chinese boxes, endlessly opening to nothing. Canetti does have an argument — and no, the book is not a work of literary criticism — but he writes from the flexible perspective of a novelist-essayist living through contemporaneity. Canetti is concrete, urgent, and humane, a writer for whom adult intelligence is of paramount importance. He is a lover of individual freedom, both his and ours, and so stresses perception of social and psychological forces as a necessary start. He does not leave behind a miasma of jargonistic prose; he still believes the truth can be approached through words; he is not book-bound. I'm sure Lee's *Savage Fields* will find defenders (Dennis Duffy's *Gardens, Covenants, Exiles* was apparently written under the watchful eyes of Mr. Lee), but his ideas are better represented in the lines of the poems gathered in *Garbage Delight*.

We come to one of the best-known "Can.Lit." thematic books, *Butterfly on Rock: A Study of Themes and Images in Canadian Literature* (1970) by D.G. Jones. Jones is a poet and a professor, and his book has had a powerful influence in academic circles and in discussions about Canadian poetry. The first sentence, however, does not entice you into reading further: "Canadians... have begun to turn back on themselves, to create that added dimension Teilhard de Chardin calls the noosphere or, to put it more simply, Canadian culture" (p. 3). A rhapsody erupts: "...more than ever before we have arrived at a point where we recognize, not only that the land is ours, but that we are the lands" (p. 3). The nationalistic note is sounded: "It is apparent that we must now move into our own cultural house, for we are no longer at home in the house of others." Northrop Frye is ritually invoked on page four. Then the rhapsody resumes: "...the voice that demands to be heard is the voice of the land" (p. 5).

Butterfly on Rock is another "text" where the theme is "a sense of exile" and "the question of feeling at home" (p. 5). The garrison mentality, the hostile wilderness, the small town versus the city, the fear of selfhood, are dutifully trooped by for our inspection as the "right" Canadian themes. These are familiar ideas today, but I'm aware how fresh they may have seemed when the study was first published. Professor Jones' writing is lucid, "lyrical," and sometimes free of nonsense. He has read widely in Canadian studies; he is fond of metaphor; and unlike his master, Frye, he seems to have a moral imagination. Jones is in fact a Romantic, nostalgic for an anthropomorphic view of nature. This view is then transformed into a political Romantic-Nationalism ("We are the lands..."). *Butterfly on Rock* is thorough in its examinations: W.O. Mitchell, Cohen, Layton, Laurence and Richler are all there. The book is provincial, indeed proudly so; Professor Jones is not in the least bit cosmopolitan, despite his repeated references to the Bible.

Still, there is an orderly intelligence at work in these pages, synthesizing disparate books and pointing out buried mythic structures. "...the world of Canadian literature," he writes, "is a kind of Old Testament world..." (p. 15). The chapter titles show this principle at work: for example, "The Sleeping Giant," "Eve in Dejection," "The Problem of Job." Jones is a mythopoeic thinker, a creator of large structural patterns.

Thus *Butterfly on Rock* is one of the most important books of criticism produced in Canada. This has nothing to do with the cogency of his thought or the quality or force of his prose. It is because his argument is *indicative*. *Butterfly on Rock* tells us about "Can.Lit." critical concerns and standards in the1970s. It tries to incite and describe "The Courage to Be."

Professor Jones' study fits a strain of thought which ignores formal questions; he scrutinizes the themes of The Land, The Small Town, The Internalized Self, and reflects on how these indicate ...what? of course... the struggle for identity. His Themes are a package set of ideas, of concepts, about the books he has read. He has in short a program to sell. Or as Professor Jones himself concludes in the ringing tones of a government cabinet minister: "Canadian, English as well as French, have arrived at the first days of Creation...." (p. 183)

Another poet-essayist is Eli Mandel. A professor as well, Mandel edited *Contexts of Canadian Criticism* (1971), providing it with a solid scholarly introduction. He writes, reflecting the defining angle of the age:

Like much else in Canadian life, Canadian literary criticism suffers from a form of national schizophrenia. It tries to find its boundaries outside itself, in some imperial world of literary tradition beyond nationality, and it seeks, both in its origins and in its development, for *an authentic identity*.... (p. 5, emphasis mine)

Mandel has written what should be regarded as a useful preliminary study of Irving Layton's poetry, called — imaginatively enough — *Irving Layton* (1969). In *Criticism: the Silent-Speaking Words* (1966) he calmly discusses the general issues of the "Nature," "Forms," and "Function"... of criticism. Mandel's volume of essays, *Another Time* (1977), shows him at work and his preference for non-systematic criticism. He is a practical critic with a strong moral bias; he does not dictate a structure to his readings: he lets his readings suggest things to him. The essays begin, sensibly, with a discussion in "The Poet as Critic" which could be subtitled "Why Criticism?" Sartre, Steiner, Wittgenstein, and Norman O. Brown file by, indicating that Professor Mandel is attuned to the modern. No nationalistic chauvinism for him. He absorbs the big issues of silence and the "death of art" in his essays "The Poet as Critic," "The Poet as Liar," and "The Language of Silence"; he discusses McLuhan, and seems aware of political and social contexts. There are insightful articles on Leonard Cohen and "The City in Canadian Poetry." He ventures the unimaginable in an interesting essay called "Banff: The Magic Mountain," by offering a brief hesitant critique of Frye. However, the whole volume suffers from Professor Mandel's penchant for assembling arguments from different sources, and then allowing everything to slip by without offering much of his own. Could this be a result of spending years in classrooms explaining other people's ideas to students?

The book cries out for a distinctive critical manner, something unexpected, polemical, challenging, allusive. As it is, *Another Time* is excruciatingly careful. No one, anywhere, could possibly be offended by what he says.

What happened? As a critic Mandel can be, in general, a conveyor of good sense, and he has laudably resisted all thematic temptations and provincial concerns to provide insights through processes of contrast. This brings up the question of what the critic's role is. To criticize is to judge. "Criticize" comes from the Latin "criticus," meaning to discern, and the Greek κρίνειν, to judge. "Crisis" derives from the same Greek root. A modern critic is a sifter who can potentially bring about a "crisis" of decision and discernment in others. "The principles of intellectual *detection* — the injunction to look *behind* everything, however trivial, in the art-field, as a matter of routine, and challenge all 'face-values' — merely have to be restated every time, for the benefit of the inattentive, and the chronically 'comfortable' — and inveterately 'cosy'."[4] This was Wyndham Lewis' opinion in 1934. From that perspective, Eli Mandel is a troubling figure. *Another Time* shows him to be sensitive and well-read; he is a better poet than others who have undertaken critical evaluations; and yet his prose remains timid and tentative. He seems to be caught in the predicament of the Canadian intellectual: Eli Mandel is a scholar, a teacher, an editor, a student of Northrop Frye's, a salesman for "Can.Lit.," and *he clearly cannot think independently*. No one can wholly escape the cultural climate, of course; but as Jacques Ellul has said, every society creates its own propaganda, and propaganda only ends with dissent. Mandel could have spoken out against the narrow nationalism of the thematic critics; he could have provided a base of opposition in the tough tradition of intellectuals like Dwight MacDonald, Irving Howe, and Alfred Kazin. He did not (for whatever reason); the price has been high; and the results are those intelligent essays in *Another Time*, especially, "Banff: the Magic Mountain," which shows him dancing and almost gagging at the end of the "Can.Lit." rope.[5]

Now a figure from the world of novel criticism, John Moss. Professor Moss has established himself with three books used inside academia and out: *Patterns of Isolation* (1974), the charmingly titled *Sex and Violence in the Canadian Novel* (1977), and *The Reader's Guide to the Canadian Novel* (1981). He has also edited anthologies like *The Canadian Novel Here and Now*, Volume I (1978) and *Beginnings*, Volume 2 (1980). He is a vague presence because his concern, he says, is for the literary form of a work and its place in the Tradition. He is also (I think) a moralist. For example: *A Reader's Guide* is an alphabetically arranged collection of remarks which show that Professor Moss is sincere; he has opinions; he has a sense of humour; he is even capable of criticizing recognized writers for their pretensions and failures. You can imagine my surprise when I flipped to the entries on Margaret Atwood and Timothy Findley. His is an erratically personal method, though, which is the custom with someone who fancies himself an outsider. Thus some of his remarks do not stand up to scrutiny, as in his reductive handling of Malcolm Lowry's complex novel, *Under the Volcano*. Professor Moss can be untrustworthy when he compares Richler with Henry Fielding or discusses Jack Hodgins without mentioning Gabriel García Márquez. He indulges in Frye-like classifications at the end, listing novels under such (inadvertently?) comic headings as "Growing Old/Being Old," and "Novels with a Significant Spiritual Dimension" (pp. 365-379). The work is meant as a Guide Book for students and teachers, and it has that indispensible "Can.Cult." attitude: enthusiasm.

Patterns of Isolation, an earlier book, has an ingenious premise: take all the clichés of National-Identity-Crisis criticism and show how true they are. Prove, that is, that "the garrison mentality" does exist as a theme in certain novels. The book begins well. Frye's name is invoked on page 15, but as someone Professor Moss disagrees with. My interest mounted. Wyndham Lewis is treated early and, unfortunately, like an uppity public-school boy who never quite learned his lesson. Professor Moss seems to be disturbed by the fact that Lewis did not appreciate Canada. Although *Self-Condemned* is rightly seen as a novel of exile, Professor

Moss soon gets ominously distracted with a windy misinterpretation of The Enemy's tactics. He neglects to point out that Exile-Isolation-Alienation are central modernist concerns; but then so do most of the other thematic critics. I could add that "Silence, exile, and cunning" was the motto of one Stephen Dedalus in a well-known book published in 1916. Also, Lewis himself, like Ezra Pound, is at the heart of the modernist dilemma: being "rootless," "a man of the world," he embodied its contradictions, its achievements, its tragic dangers. Professor Moss proceeds through the forms of "Canadian" exile, which he categorizes as "garrison," "frontier," "colonial," "immigrant." He analyzes the delicate complexities of that classic static book of "Can.Lit." courses, *As For Me and My House.* He demonstrates that he is adept at close readings. He shows a proper regard for the interaction of character and environment, although he neglects to adequately define what he means by environment (is it natural? urban? suburban? electronic?). He also shows a fondness for bizarre comparisons, like Sinclair Ross with Marcel Proust. He makes grand claims: "Canadian fiction is rich with individual characters in isolation from conventional reality" (p. 239). We could call this *solipsism,* for that is his hidden theme: the intense self-absorption of the Canadian literary scene. Professor Moss writes of "national being" (whatever that is), and we realize that *Patterns of Isolation* is very much in the Great "Can.Lit." Vain. Still, his interrogations of certain novels are sometimes suggestive.

On the other hand, we have *Sex and Violence in the Canadian Novel, The Ancestral Present,* and here things get murky. The opening sentences are pure hyperbole: "Literature... is not a specialty like gardening or harness racing, but is the most vital nourishment of our civilization" (p. 5). And: "Those who dismiss fiction injure themselves and dismiss the better part of humanity." That these are unsolicited clichés unsupported by any argument does not appear to bother the author. If it doesn't bother him, why should it bother us? Then the question starts nagging at you: who is this book for?

Moving on: Professor Moss shows that he has a few modish fixations: "During this contemporary or post-modern era...." [Should "contemporary" be capitalized? No. How about "post-modern"? Or just "modern"? Is Professor Moss assuming a stage beyond literary modernism? Are we to think of Barth, Barthes, Borges, and Barthelme? What assumption lies behind this remark?] "...the Canadian novel has coalesced into an imposing representative of our national community...." [Fanfare.] "...in world literature, distinguished as a whole by its apparent affinity for sex and violence..." [Those good grey Canadians with an affinity for sex and violence? He must be pulling our collective leg. Note the qualifier before "affinity."] "...particularly as they relate..." [Ah, the reassuring bow to the *Zeitgeist* with "relate."] "...to divers matters of identity" [And there it is, the reflexive theme.]

Several perceptive declarations follow: "Sex and sexuality have many meanings," and "All literary endeavour is in some measure political" (p. 6). Professor Moss concludes his Preface with a list of evaluations that resemble awards handed out at a literary merit night: "The great Canadian novel is..."; "The most exquisitely accomplished experimental novel is..."; "The most lyrical..."; "The most inventive..."; "The most consistently accomplished, original and influential storyteller of our time and place is..." (pp. 6-7). These pronouncements could inspire savage satire: instead, the reader should recite them out loud for himself sometime, preferably with the closing bars of Wagner's Overture to *Tännhauser* playing *molto fortissimo*.

In the following chapter Professor Moss pursues his ideas about sex and violence, showing how Canadian novels fit into "the Great Tradition," examining works by Scott Symons and Matt Cohen. Then the exasperating declarations surface again: "There almost certainly is a higher incidence of sex and violence in the Canadian novel than elsewhere..." (p. 29). Surely he is mistaken. Greater sex and violence than *Last Exit to Brooklyn*, *Candy*, or *Naked Lunch*? Or anything by Jean Genet? Is this supposed to be Professor Moss' *mad* book? If not, then who is it for? Students? Teachers? The Canada Council? Those who know a lot about literature will be impatient with this sort of statement, and those who do not will be misled. You are therefore left with the feeling that this study was meant to be iconoclastic as it seems to indicate a wild desire to break away from the usual solemnity of academic writing.

Professor Moss explores his thematic threads in the works of Alice Munro, Margaret Laurence, Ernest Buckler and Robertson Davies, among others. For all his specialized knowledge of Canadian fiction, I read with growing frustration. I realize this is a work of literary criticism, but how seriously are we to take a book that analyzes sex and violence and hardly mentions Freud, and doesn't mention Dostoyevsky, Henry Miller, D.H. Lawrence or Wilhelm Reich at all? Here is one of Professor Moss' bewildering remarks: "A Freudian analayst [*sic*, unless it's a pun] - critic would undoubtedly have a field day with the Deptford trilogy" (p. 122).

Given that *Sex and Violence* may be Professor Moss' attempt to be Leslie Fiedler (notorious opponent of the American literary establishment and author of *Love and Death in the American Novel*), his book comes perilously close to "lit.crit." preciousness.

Now, why am I going on like this about books most readers will not bother with? No matter how scrupulous a writer is, someone will catch him on something. These "Can.Lit." veterans, however, have no one who is looking after them. They have created an insular atmosphere and are patrolling that small territory with considerable licence. Worse, there are readers-writers-publishers-editors inside and outside the classroom who are vulnerable to their conceptual framework.

In this case, Professor Moss has been a shock. It is disturbing to watch a sometimes acerbic and certainly good-natured critic enrolling as a salesman. He concludes in "Gathering the Canadian Identity" with a confusing discussion of critical principles, ending with the idea of the "pure" critic as "guru, guide, and impresario" (p. 312), and a redundancy ("This is a study of the Canadian novel..."). Professor Moss redeems himself several years later with an essay in *The Human Element II* (1981) called "Bushed in the Sacred Wood." Here he declares what he may have secretly felt when he wrote *Sex and Violence*:

> The resources of English Canadian literary criticism are no longer adequate to the achievement of the literature. The boom years of Canadian self-consciousness have passed and sales of Canadian books are down, critical commentary is in a state of exhaustion. Responses that were apparently valid only a short time ago now seem inappropriate and often at odds with the function of criticism.[6]

This is honest, and his defensive survey of Canadian criticism is not optimistic. Honesty is a sign of the ability to truly re-evaluate. And if Moss is right about his gloom, then you sense the uneasiness the "Can.Lit." cabals feel when they gaze back on the halcyon days of rampant nationalism and what happened to their ability to judge and discern. You can also see why the standards of dialogue between writer, reader, and critic have sunk to the state that they have in Canada. We may also understand why the "Can.Lit." phenomenon (or "Canned Lit.," as it has been referred to) has little support outside the universities and the editors of small magazines.*

---

* I do not mean that Canadian readers are not interested in their writers. They are. I am talking about the "Can.Lit." designation as it applies to a particular squad of scholars, critics, and authors.

The writer Professor Moss proposes as a model of critical acuity is George Woodcock. Others agree. "In the past, I have claimed that there are three fine Canadian critics," David Helwig writes in *The Human Elements I* (1978), "George Woodcock, George Woodcock, George Woodcock."[7] Superlatives aside, Mr. Woodcock has held an important position because of his groundbreaking work with *Canadian Literature*, his prodigious output, and his genial "non-aligned" status. "Prodigious output" is an understatement. George Woodcock is an industry. But since I cannot cover everything he has written, I'll concentrate on those books which are relevant here.

Odysseus Ever Returning: Essays on Canadian Writers and Writing (1970), despite its portentous mythic title, is one of Mr. Woodcock's better collections. In "Away from Lost Worlds," he perceptively discusses "the lack of a true literary world" in Canada (p. 2). He reflects on the institutional influence of the CBC and the Canada Council. He criticizes Morley Callaghan and Hugh MacLennan. He is blunt: "Regional novels that rise above sentimental pseudo-history or amiable rusticity are rare in Canada" (p. 7). His essay on Wyndham Lewis' tragic sojourn in Canada, "Momaco Revisited," recognizes Lewis as an exiled Canadian whose audience was European. The essay on Layton, "A Grab at Proteus," is one of the better surveys of a prolific poet. Woodcock is an expert on general surveys: that is his primary method of investigation.

Woodcock's prose, at its best, can be informal, steady and warm. He combines technical analysis with a sense of socio-political contexts, and examines the author's personality and the effect of his work on readers. His own attitudes towards criticism can be found in "Views of Canadian Criticism," where he quotes D.S. Savage: "The routine work of criticism is to interpret, elucidate and evaluate our literature and in so doing to define, defend and expound the tradition" (p. 130). He defines cosmopolitanism as an "interplay of various traditions" (p. 131), of both the local and the universal. Joyce had to live in Europe to reconstruct Dublin. That is cultural interplay. Woodcock's approach is eclectic and non-thematic, and thus he offers an alternative to the closed systems Frye constructs and to the thematic critics.

At some point, however, George Woodcock went from being a distanced but sympathetic essayist in the tradition of journalist-critics like George Orwell and V.S. Pritchett, to the leading "Can.Lit." salesman. Turning from *Odysseus Ever Returning* to *The*

World of Canadian Writing (1980) is like jumping from solid land into quicksand. The book's introduction shows that Woodcock can still be disarmingly personable. He chats amiably about what has happened in "Can.Lit." over the last thirty years. He is, he claims, the premier witness.

We read and start happening upon the right Canadian critical notes — "urban" (disaster! p. 8), "rural," "the invasion of American junk-cult" (p. 8), and finally the stamp of a nationalist critic: "And behind it all [the literary community], the great forms of the land remain, unchanged and slowly impressing themselves on one's consciousness, so that to recognize them on returning is to enter an inner as well as outer landscape" (p. 8). And behind this you can hear the echoes of D.G. Jones, Dennis Lee and George Grant.

Mr. Woodcock then becomes enamoured with himself:

> And suddenly, with Proustian brightness as I read the letters, memories began to sparkle like fireflies on the edge of a dark wood and I thought it was time to start writing my autobiography after all and give these early years in Canada their proper vividness. (p. 10)

Proceeding through Mr. Woodcock's surveys, his mind guiding us "with Proustian brightness" (and with his sentences certainly getting longer), we come across a reversal like: "There is no writer other than MacLennan whom one could plausibly consider the Canadian Balzac" (p. 34). And then a bombshell:

> Did we — could we — have a Canadian equivalent to Tolstoy? My answer...was immediate: Yes, Margaret Laurence! ...Afterwards, as I thought about what Tolstoy means to me and compared that with what Margaret Laurence means to me... I was tempted to elevate my answer from the status of a rash impulse to that of a flash of insight. (p. 40)... Margaret Laurence positively resembles Tolstoy in possessing the panoramic sense of space and history.... (p. 43)

I admire Margaret Laurence's novels, but I cannot see how this majestic comparison can be of benefit to anyone. It is like comparing a modest folk song to a Mahler symphony. Mr. Woodcock follows up with an insightful review of Laurence's work, yet his generalizations create the impression that he has to outdo the other critics with his praise and write the jacket blurbs for Laurence's next book. This does not make a good atmosphere for intelligent debate, as it does Laurence a disservice and betrays a dangerous feeling of insecurity expressing itself in premature eulogizing.

The essay on Laurence, "The Human Elements," reveals George Woodcock's colours. There are things to admire: his tenacity and generosity, his non-dogmatic stance, and his occasional eloquence. There are also things to abjure: the self-congratulatory air, his long-winded prose and over-zealous generalizations, as if uncritical enthusiasm alone were enough to inspire a mood of urgent dialogue and the recognition of literary value.

The strangest for last: John Fekete's *The Critical Twilight: Explorations in the Ideology of Anglo-American Literary Theory from Eliot to McLuhan* (1977). A genuine Marxist critic on the Canadian scene is certainly an oddity, and *The Critical Twilight* traces the collapse of criticism, or, rather, its betrayal to scholasticism and amoral standards, from T.S. Eliot to Frye and McLuhan. Even if the entire book is cast in "the criticism of criticism" mode, it has passionate rage and a cosmopolitan reach. Unfortunately, Professor Fekete has trouble with the English language. His prose is humourless, turgid, and studded with polysyllabic abstractions like "particularization," "interiority," "positivity," "indeterminations," "periodization," "superordination," and "refrangibility"; he uses theoretic catch-words like "praxis" and "reification"; and he has a special fetish for "fetish."

Here are two fairly typical examples of the prose: "A thorough analysis of McLuhan's cybernetic semiotic, and its relations with social, historical, and mental life, challenges on the ontological level McLuhan's counterrevolutionary religion of deified technological transcendence..." (p. xxiv); and: "In Ransom, the fetish of disinterested contemplative cognition truncates the aesthetic dialectic at the point of suspension of pragmatic immediacy via the medium." (p. 81) I am not quoting out of context, for, unlike Frederic Jameson and Herbert Marcuse who use Marxist and Freudian terminology for a tactical effect of reader dislocation, Professor Fekete seems dazzled by the opaque rhetoric and pseudo-scientific jargon of the Frankfurt school. This is distracting. His selection of critics is also idiosyncratic, and perhaps coy. He places Eliot, Ransom, and Frye in a direct lineage, and (deliberately?) neglects D.H. Lawrence, F.R. Leavis, Lewis, and Pound. As you might expect, the best Marxists are there, like Georg Lukács, Ernst Fischer and Walter Benjamin, and he shares their sense of historical determinism and class struggle.

Nevertheless, there is something to admire in *The Critical Twilight*. Professor Fekete's method is surprisingly perceptive. Frye and McLuhan are included as extensions and modifications of earlier intellectual trends. He spurns provincialism, and thankfully, the "Can.Cult." club is never mentioned. He misreads McLuhan because he does not understand satire; but then misinterpreting McLuhan is an easy thing to do, especially for a critic who is an ideologue. Still, Fekete's interrogation is based on a committed and courageous social concern: he wants to see what the effect of these critics' ideas and practices has been on intelligent research and discrimination. For those writers who have turned inward, into the literary text itself, Fekete's tough moral stand works wonders. His critique of Northrop Frye is shrewd and useful, although, again, the view of the dialectical critic seeking an alternative synthesis to Frye's. I found myself in partial agreement with most of what he says about literary discussion since the 1930s: Professor Fekete attacks its wilful abstracting and self-referential tendencies, its contempt for the world, its escape from factual apprehension. He shows that current intellectual anaemia has been the result of an inability to see that fiction, poetry, and drama are not autonomous systems that require microscopic de-constructions or reconstructions on computer charts. Literature is not reality: it is an argument with reality.

As *The Critical Twilight* has a dense derivative style and a too rigid ideological posture, it is destined for a small audience, which is unfortunate, as the argument invites a measure of debate by enfolding its theoretical apparatus around a consistent line of political-economic reasoning. He performs what F.R. Leavis once called a "valuable stimulus to disagreement." And whether you are sympathetic to his political affinities or not, John Fekete is a real critic, dedicated to castigating apathy, fads, and the unstated biases of those literary mandarins who dwell in the thin air of ethereal realms.

Enough. My acclimatization was not meant to be definitive, but what I have surveyed should indicate the mood of things. In the end, you are left with feelings of squander and misdirection, good intentions but slack results. I'm forced to ask: has there ever been a truly critical spirit in the country? The questions I raise concern the authenticity and vitality of a writer and the relevance of his observations. You should be able to trust a writer's energy and intelligence, even when that author is suffering from what Irving Howe termed "the generosity of confusion."

When we are reading we should be asking: is the writer making an approach to the truth? does he have the power to make words grip reality? is there a sense of grit and guidance? What is missing from almost every one of the writers I have examined is the pressure of debate, the drive of dissatisfaction. What is particularly disturbing is that when many of these poets and novelists turn to criticism, *they do not criticize at all*: their thinking turns to mush; they write nervous propaganda; they slip on thematic strait-jackets; apologia, panegyric and mythopoeia become the dominant modes of approach.

Which leads me to emergency remedies. No quick cure is possible for such a large ailing beast. From our examination of the principal players, it is obvious that some extremes may be necessary. Nietzsche resorted to "philosophizing with a hammer" when he realized that the philsophical methods of his time were decadent. If we hammer at anything it should be the way to achieve standards and dialogue and perception. "Good manners are the sign of a dull literary age."[8] How true. The scholars toil over footnotes, extending the ledgers of academic commentary while the thematic writers can barely manage a good polemic. (If the universities decided to discontinue "Can.Lit." studies, would Canadian writing wither away?). Any extreme would be unfair — as everything is in the quotidian — and unpopular with those who are insecure over whether Canadian literature is as good as anyone else's. But the point in Canadian writing is surely writing: it is energy, feeling, and experience shaped through language and mind. The writer criticizes fiction, poetry, and the essay, in order to create vital art. The question of a Canadian Theme cannot be imposed: it can only develop. As T.S. Eliot said, there is no substitute for intelligence and wide reading, but when the prevailing ideas are stuffed in classrooms you have to take steps to think for yourself.

Finally: self-definition is an arduous task, if we need reminding. It takes time, insight, discipline, and most importantly, intellectual honesty. No amount of government money, media advice or cultural propaganda can create "instant art" or "character." Moreover, modern literature springs from individuals who are in a relationship of *tension* and *discovery* with their environment, their history, their words, and themselves. False meanings and false hopes divert this search for understanding, leaving temporary enthusiasms, the romance of idealistic nationalism, a complacent sense of self. Certainly, much of modern writing is preoccupied with self-worth: the issue of what is humane action, of what is personality, of what is reality, possesses artists and intellectuals to an extraordinary degree. Under the threat of instant annihilation, these questions loom large. The Master-Builders of the Canadian Theme, huddled indoors to keep warm against the battering cold, refuse to see that the desire for definition and the struggle for voice are universal urges. The problem has never been Canadian identity, but human identity. You need only look at the best of contemporary writing, from Czeslaw Milosz and Tadeusz Konwicki to Milan Kundera, from Saul Bellow and the late John Cheever to Ted Hughes, Anthony Burgess, and Doris Lessing (before her science-fiction series, *Canopus in Argos: Archives*), from Octavio Paz to García Márquez (particularly in *Chronicle of a Death Foretold*), to see that their work reflects concerns with the collision of the ethical with technology and society, with the confrontation between the human spirit and destructive ideology, between the individual and the mass, between the role of the artist and the consumer society, between history and change, between the word and the electric charge, between cultural memory and spiritual impoverishment, between the authentic person and the ghost-images of the present. The important Canadian artists and thinkers, like Marshall McLuhan, Irving Layton, Glenn Gould, John Kenneth Galbraith, Margaret Laurence, Mordecai Richler, Marie-Clair Blais and (even) Margaret Atwood, have been dealing with these situations with degrees of perceptive and formal success. (Or they have been suffering from the effect of these factors, and perhaps unwittingly, as with Leonard Cohen.) But some authors do not wish to give shape to their world with words. They avoid the calling of the age, the audience, and the Tradition. They choose nostalgic myth and nationalism, or rush into "the Gameness of Game," and avoid the exacting terms of the contract with existence. Writing helps to make us human: we are "the language animal." Whatever we write and read should stand up to the question of what it means to be alive now. Then the examinations can begin. Then a true involvement in our time.

(1982-83)

Part Three

Raging Bull:
The Poetry, Politics and Polemics of
Irving Layton

The isolation of the artist (which frequently assumes the form of the most brazen publicity-minded exhibitionism) is inevitable at a time when action and knowledge tread two separate paths and meet only by chance....

Wherever we look we see a rush towards imitation and anonymity, and it would be absurd to expect that when the collective block has reached its grade of maximum solidity, the very idea of an individual art, or of any sort of art, should seem anything other than outrageous.

Eugenio Montale

Niagara-on-the-Lake, September 1982:

> Three fudge stores
> two bookstores
> a clean library uncontaminated
> by *Commentary* and *Encounter*
> English beer
> English biddies
> The Prince of Wales
> The Buttery
> tourist shops on both sides
> of Queen Street
> selling Canadian identity bracelets

Grey clouds, drizzle, and slippery streets. It is early fall and already there is the feel of a cool November. The main street is devoid of people: its mood is antique and artificial. It is hard to believe that Irving Layton, a poet commonly regarded as the Raging Bull of Canadian Letters, lives here among

vinyards, orchards, and Orangemen
and a tower clock
that rings out the hours
and tells everyone
when to stop yawning
and go to bed.[1]

His house is on a sidestreet. It is set back in the trees, a few blocks from the Shaw Festival Theatre. He greets me in the driveway. His appearance is that of a poet's: wild white hair, a large expressive face, sly alive eyes, a head that seems too wide for the humped shoulders, short body. He darts toward me, slightly stooped, his eyes appraising, stretching out his arms in a way that could be construed as either a gesture of welcome or a signal that he is about to pounce. Inside, he bustles around the kitchen pouring drinks, enquiring after health, movies, books, travel plans, refilling my glass (repeatedly), sitting down to read a poem that he has just dashed off, or so he says. He wears a faded plaid shirt, grey soiled pants that are bulging and creased, with frayed suspenders holding them up. A mask: he looks vaguely like a poeticizing peasant.

The conversation turns quickly toward the question of exile: "I don't think it's a good idea for a poet to be an expatriate," he says. "He has his roots in his nation. It doesn't matter if he loves or hates his country." He lights an enormous cigar. "You see, I know this place...." A puff, a cloud of smoke. "It gave me what I needed. A theme. Security. I knew what to fight...." His head trembles slightly. "There were times when I thought about leaving," he says, using his cigar to punctuate his sentences, "but they were brief. — America? No. The United States is not hospitable to poets. Lowell, Berryman, Pound, Delmore Schwartz. Well, I've had a good living in Canada. Teaching is my great love other than writing. I wouldn't have had the same advantages elsewhere."

When I ask him about his wild reputation in Canadian literary circles, he laughs, and replies in a soft voice: "I'm not performing when I'm alone. But performing in public is a complicated thing. It's not a question of inauthenticity or sincerity. And yet sometimes when you see yourself... it's like seeing yourself in a coffin. There's such a distortion. What you get is a selection. It's even true of my books. Can I be reduced to my poems? No, because I select them too. And I've written so many now...."

He leans back in his chair and talks as if he were alone and addressing something beyond the window: "Today the image counts for everything. It separates and distorts and reduces you to a moment. And sometimes my image is all that people know...."

Suddenly he picks up the cigar, flicks off its ashes and thrusts it into his mouth. Then he says: "Take it from an old poet... all that sustains *me* is lust and rage...."

Thus Irving Layton in his seventy-first year, taking a brief break from himself. On another occasion one year later, Layton spoke in what is for many a familiar voice: "The true poet is a prophet. His vocation is that of someone who is passionately concerned with the fate, fortune, and adventure of the human spirit.... Looking back, I would say I am in the Hebrew tradition of prophesying. I consider myself not the equal but certainly the successor to the Hebrew prophets of the Old Testament.... Everything I have written has been animated by this religious vocation of mine. For me, there has been a constant *engagement* with reality, and it's been a long, complex, and sometimes very difficult journey."[2]

These encounters suggest that interpretation of Layton's role, work, and personality is fraught with danger. For a poet who presents a unified point-of-view, a humane poetic, who is the author of over forty books, twice nominated for the Nobel Prize, and one of the only literary artists in Canada who is durable and readable, it is fascinating to realize that Layton's name provokes a near-riot of adulatory and dismissive reactions. Why did he take an exposed public route? If we are to make accurate evaluations of his presence we should begin here:

> Poetry, dearly as I have loved it, has always been to me but a divine plaything. I never attached any great value to poetical fame, and I trouble myself very little whether people praise my verses or blame them. But lay on my coffin a sword; for I was a brave soldier in the war of liberation of humanity.[3]

This is Heinrich Heine (1797-1856), although the combination of bravado, bluster and polemical fervour is virtually the Layton signature. Heine's relationship with the German culture of his time bears similarities to the war Layton waged with Canadian poets, critics and readers. Indeed, the author of the above declaration is someone who wished to be remembered as *more than a poet*.

Layton has assumed the stance of a self-proclaimed prophet and historian, a one-man "god-intoxicated" army out to teach the

"philistines and gentility"[4] the necessity of creative energy.
Despite his lyrical gifts, Layton's art is never just art. In fact it often
seems as if he doesn't care about art. His concern has been for what
Heine calls "the war of liberation" to create a "non-alienated
man," a fight for political, poetical, sexual freedom, forged in what
you could call his ideology of joy.   He has had a consistent view
of what human society should be and what an artist must say about
contemporary history, and he has followed this vision from the
publication of *Here and Now* in 1946 through every poem, lecture
and essay. The conscious vulgarization of his mask and his poetic
style, his use of the available means of communication — the
classroom and lecture hall; appearances on *Fighting Words*;
editorials to newspapers; the same interview said over and over —
were part of a strategy of radical change. He has pursued the role
of the authentic voice in a time of dissolving and uncertain
identities. As a result, Layton's best lyrics are the most
indispensible of any Canadian poet of his generation. The result
has also been appalling. For Layton's final entrapment in his role
and the *consistency* of his approach had a devastating effect on his
writings, especially his prose. However, his model of what a poet
must do is central to our understanding of Canadian writing.

II

"What is a poet?" Wordsworth asked in his Preface to the second
edition of *Lyrical Ballads* (1800). "He is a man speaking to men... a
man pleased with his own passions and volitions, and who rejoices
more than other men in the spirit of life that is in him...."[5] Thus a
poet sets out to redefine his terms of reference. Of course, a long
history of English poetry and polemics preceded the publication
of that Romantic manifesto, so Wordsworth knew his words'
worth, as it were. He could be certain that serious readers would
understand why the question was asked. Imagine another cultural
context: after the modernist "renaissance," post-World War II,
after the holocaust, the European *suicide*, as Wyndham Lewis
called it, when Ezra Pound is incarcerated in an insane asylum,
when the audience has shifted its attention to movies, music and
TV, when anti-art and non-art rule, when the dadaist's put-on has
become the nihilist's zero. What, then, is a poet? Add further
complications: a place without a flag to identify as its own, whose
"Literature" (it cannot be called writing yet) is either imported or
institutionalized, where someone can poeticize:

Dere's somet'ing stirrin' ma blood tonight,
 On de night of de young new year,
W'ile de camp is warm an' de fire is bright,
 An' de bottle is close at han'...[6]

And it could be considered a part of the national treasury. So:
what is the writer's role? where is the audience? who are the
enemies? what forms and styles are vital and available? is the poet
to ally himself with "that timeless European mythology" or with
the American Idiom?[7] There are other poet-pioneers forging their
way, like E.J. Pratt, F.R. Scott, Dorothy Livesay, and Earle
Birney; but they do not provide the model you want, which must
be "realistic, contemporary, circumstantial, critical, exploratory."[8]

A writer has to *feel* time, as the poét Eugenio Montale has
said, meaning that every age has an internal rhythm, a pulse, a
tone, to which the responsive artist must attend. The situation the
writer finds himself in (partially) determines his sense of vocation.
Vocation is voice, a tuning in. Layton felt that what he could offer,
given his Jewish-Montreal background and his particular talent,
was the poetic of a man speaking about "common" things, a
poetry of real events, raw experience. He rejected the Symbolists'
private speech (the runic route through Mallarmé), rejected the
conservative traditionalism of Eliot, absorbed the polemical spirit
of Pound and Shaw, absorbed the idea of a vulgar American idiom
("vulgar": "vulgate": meaning "of the common people"). "I am
on the side of the great vulgarians," he said.[9] And he hammered
out what he claimed was unique: the poetic of a Nietzschean man,
"The Swimmer," a new land's voice and mask, part European
and part North American, with the populist avowal "to write
poems/ that can be read/ by/ butchers/ and/ bankers." Through
the force of his imagination and will, Layton tried to breach the
barriers of historical disaster, "gentility," and colonial isolation.

Unknown to most, Layton's intellectual training was
skeptical, liberal, and rationalist: his MA thesis was in Political
Science, its subject — "Harold Laski: The Paradoxes of a Liberal
Marxist" (a short version of it appears in *Taking Sides*, pages 21-
40). He has read deeply in philosophy, politics, and history; he is
conscious of where ideology can lead in practical affairs. Unlike
those writers who began publishing in the 1960s, Layton was not
self-consciously "literary." But the poetic "daimons" (his word)
never leave anyone in a unified sober state. As Layton writes in the
Foreword to *Europe and other Bad News* (1979): "With my first
published book *Here and Now*, I began a dialogue with my

compatriots concerning the nature of poetry, its mad intention to pick the Deity's brains and present his vision of reality."[10] Layton insists that he prefers his writers "mad": hence his preference for Heine over Goethe, Blake over Wordsworth, D.H. Lawrence over just about anybody. That is an easy thing *to say*. However, when a writer launches a career in a country locked in a deadly stasis, then madness seems necessary.

What does the poet become, then? "...a poet is one who explores new areas of sensibility," Layton writes in *Engagements* (1972). "If he has the true vocation he will take risks, for him there can be no 'dogmatic slumbers'" (p. 87). The poet is the devourer of experience. He will not be afraid to appear ferocious or foolish, a Machiavellian individualist who engages society and insists on his visionary centrality. As Layton says in a self-revealing lecture, "Prince Hamlet and the Beatniks" (1962): "Like the Hebrew prophets he has to storm... He cannot go underground. He cannot exhibit cowardice. He may not retreat. He must constantly attempt to enlighten his fellowmen, his contemporaries, and point out to them *the defects of their society*, and never discourage them by saying, 'the situation is well nigh hopeless....'"[11] The writer counters despair with celebration and accusation: he throws open the doors and says: "look... *life*."

Layton's arrival in the quiet literary circle was not heralded by trumpets. The reception of his early books shows Canadian culture at its insensitive worst. In the late 1940s he was referred to as "a steam boiler," "a pseudo-Whitman," "a noisy hot-gospeller" by Northrop Frye, "a star... of unquestioned brightness and constancy" by A.M. Klein. It was the American poet and editor Robert Creeley who called him "the first great Canadian poet." The battle continued, as later he was acknowledged as "a real poet" by Northrop Frye, "a backwoodsman" by William Carlos Williams in his introduction to the first volume of Layton's poetry published in the United States, "a Promethean liberator" by Layton's friend and *First Statement* colleague, Louis Dudek, "a benevolent Caliban, father, historian, a tavern wit" by Hugh Kenner, who wrote an introduction to a collection of Layton's poems published by James Laughlin's New Directions. Layton remained "out in the wilderness" as he describes it until 1959, when McClelland and Stewart published *A Red Carpet for the Sun*. During the 1960s and early '70s greater recognition came, as he is called "the official braggart of Canadian letters," "the Lusty Laureate from the Slums," "the Canadian Hemingway," "a legend" by Charles Bukowski, "a Raging Ego," "a literary troglodyte" (Louis Dudek's revised polemical attack in 1965), "a first rate whistler" "a poet in the old Romantic sense," in George Woodcock's belatedly revised opinion. In the late 1970s and early '80s, Layton had achieved the status of an institution: he was "the Acceptable Variant," "a heroic vitalist," "an ass" according to Susan Musgrave, and "an orator howling in an empty stadium," in the words of Kingston Laureate, David Helwig.

Throughout those years Layton's campaign was parodied and patronized (in Aviva Layton's *Nobody's Daughter*, the poet bursts into a bookstore like a veritable symbol of the Life-Force, shouting "Nietzsche... Give me Nietzsche!"); scolded and savaged (an article in 1982 accuses Layton of being chauvinistic and immoral, in short worse than the author, lesser than the readers; George Bowering writes in a poem "I can't imagine him actually/ I can't imagine him ＿＿＿ a woman or a/ boy"[2]); exalted and exonerated ("a poet of genius," Al Purdy sighs; "I had to leave the country to understand his value," George Woodcock admits; the author of thirty-six indisputably great poems, a correspondent allows); imitated and acknowledged (dozens of poets and poems bear his editorial mark), and ignored and acclaimed (a reading in October 1982 at Toronto's Harbourfront was only half-attended; that same year he was nominated for the Nobel Prize by the Italians and the South Koreans). Layton has thrived on and been wounded by these generally trivializing perceptions. But then he is a lover of paradox and a born performer who is anti-intellectual and yet well-read; anti-academic and yet a professor of literature at two universities; anti-nationalist and yet has remained most of his life in Canada; anti-Wasp and yet has lived in Niagara-on-the-Lake and Oakville, in the heartland of Upper Canada; anti-Communist and yet a former Marxist with enduring Socialist sympathies; anti-feminist and yet a lover of women ("Women are to me what daffodils were to Wordsworth"); anti-"Can.Lit." and yet an ardent supporter of young writers. To which I could add the following paradoxical poses noted in volumes like *The Shattered Plinths*, *The Covenant*, and *Droppings from Heaven*: progressive-reactionary, mystical-existential, unsentimental-nostalgic, ribald-decorous, amoral-didactic, clumsy-elegant, realistic-idealistic.

A mass of contradictions? Call it the *mask* of controversy: the committed poet, at once lover, buffoon and prophet, "a walking blasphemy" who shows all the emotions from malice and ecstasy, showing that the artist is part of what Thomas Carlyle described in "The Hero as Man of Letters" as "a perpetual Priesthood, from age to age, teaching all men that God is still present in their life;

that all 'Appearance', whatsoever we see in the world is but as a vesture for the 'Divine Idea of the World', for 'that which lies at the bottom of Appearance'. In the true Literary Man there is thus ever, acknowledged by the world, a sacredness: he is the light of the world; the world's Priest; — guiding it, like a sacred pillar of Fire, in its dark pilgrimage."[13]

Such are the contours of his outrageous career. But what of the poems behind the heroic mask, the war with the philistines, and the public distortions?

III

So "a man speaking to men" about persona, passions, place and process:

> By walking I found out
> Where I was going
>
> By intensely hating, how to love.
> By loving, whom and what to love....
>
> Out of infirmity, I have built strength.
> Out of untruth, truth.
> From hypocrisy, I weave directness.
>
> Almost now I know who I am.
> Almost I have the boldness to be that man....
>   ("There Were No Signs")[14]

An attic style — succinct, vigorous, graceful — adjusted to suit an ideal of direct communication:

> Struck
> the bull calf drew in his thin forelegs
> as if gathering strength for a mad rush...
> tottered... raised his darkening eyes to us,
> and I saw we were at the far end
> of his frightened look, growing smaller and smaller...
>   (The Bull Calf")

Though the style is dramatic, there is nothing that you could not under some circumstances actually say:

I placed
my hand
upon
her thigh.

By the way
she moved
away
I could see
her devotion
to literature
was not
perfect.
   (Misunderstanding")

In the above poems there is an implied listener. In poems like
"Where Was Your Shit-Detector, Pablo?," "Osip Mandelstam
(1881-1940)," "The New Sensibility,"[15] and "With Undiminished
Fire" (for Louis Dudek),[16] the poet addresses writers he feels
affinities for and the reader is invited to overhear:

Pablo, I can't help liking someone
who gets excited about injustice and ass,
who makes clever feints against Death,
and asks everyone to admire
his deft trickery and showmanship.
You're a poet with panache
and the ladies must have adored you.
But where was your shit-detector
when it came to Stalin
and his evil-smelling crew?

Despite the calculated crudities ("ass," "shit-detector"), the
language is "fine." These poems are never flat or monotone-ish.
The rhythm follows the drive, the suspense, of the voice. The
image or attitude dictates the rhetorical shape, which in Layton's
case is invariably *a dialogue*. Conversation poems, we could call
them, after Coleridge.
  Yet you can feel the intake and exhalation of breath in these
lines. Layton's poetic is one of power. His rhythms are physical,
aggressive. He never withdraws, he pushes out:

The afternoon foreclosing, see
The swimmer plunges from his raft,
Opening the spray corollas by his act of war —
The snake heads strike
Quickly and are silent.
    ("The Swimmer")

Layton is a student of power and apocalypse. Hence the violence of his imagery, the extreme passions of his blastings and blessings, the obsession with figures like Hitler and Stalin. He writes with precision about the infatuation with murder and authority, because he understands how power can destroy and reveal the spirit. Witness the remarkable and chilling poem, "The Shark," which describes the allure of the abyss:

In some quiet bay
or deserted inlet
he is waiting for me...

I want him to be black, wholly black
I want him to be famished and solitary
I want him to be quietly ready for me
as if he were the angel of death

The last thing I want my alive eyes
to behold before I close them forever
are his ripsaw teeth.

The animals he writes about reflect his concerns with cunning and will: they are almost always reptiles, snakes, sharks, or foxes, cats and whales. His understanding of power also makes him sensitive to suffering and victims, "those to whom things are done."

    In modern writing, the apocalyptic-romantic line runs through D.H. Lawrence and Ted Hughes in England to Jack Kerouac, Allen Ginsberg and Norman Mailer in the United States. There is another line, which we could call satirical-classical, that moves through Pound, Eliot, Lewis, and Joyce. If Layton's poems fit anywhere, it is with the apocalyptic-romantics; but these are decadent times when the hard line of rectitude has dissolved, so we find Layton writing love lyrics after Sappho, satire after Juvenal, elegies after Catallus. Layton is an *apocalyptic-satirist*, because for all his image as "a backwoodsman," he is a classical craftsman. In the following, high rhetorical diction and allusion are combined with common-places, puns, and deflating ironies:

Whatever else poetry is freedom.
Forget the rhetoric, the trick of lying
All poets pick up sooner or later. From the river.
Rising like the thin voice of castratos — the mist;
Poplars and pines grow straight but oaks are gnarled;
Old codgers must speak of death, boys break windows,
Women lie honestly by their men at last.
("Whatever Else Poetry is Freedom")

What distinguishes these poems is the tone. Layton can mimic a mincing "poetaster," a scorned rival, or a favourite model like Byron, but it is that singular human tone which is identifiably his. Layton does not anthologize well because no poem can represent the process of *the voice*. This enormous willed confidence has allowed Layton late into his life to churn out the same poetry as if he were turning them out on a photocopier. Thus we can move from "The Swimmer" to "The Wheel" in *A Wild Peculiar Joy* (1982), from *A Laughter in the Mind* (1958) to the poems in *The Gucci Bag* (1983), and observe how little development there is. The rhythms are more exact; the control is firm. But the transformations and disintegration we find in, say, Ezra Pound's tumultuous career, in the leap from *Personae* to "Drafts and Fragments" in *The Cantos*, is not evident in Layton's. Nor is metamorphosis important. What is humanly there, will always be there. *When he changes at all, "the unwavering eye" changes its focus of attention.*
This means Layton wants his poems to be read as part of one long work. The unity of his movement can be seen in *A Wild Peculiar Joy*; there is a distinct narrative thrust. Note the placement of "The Birth of Tragedy," its title taken from Nietzsche's first important essay:

And me happiest when I compose poems.
  Love, power, the huzza of battle
  are something, are much
yet a poem includes them like a pool
  water and reflection.
In me, nature's divided things —
  tree, mould on tree —
  have their fruition;

I am their core. Let them swap,
  bandy, like a flame swerve.
I am their mouth; as a mouth I serve.

The first five lines are the anchors of his vision; "happiness" in creation; "love," "power," "the huzza of battle" all contained in art. Poetry is the ultimate power because it is the power of the imagination to transform. Flipping to eight pages from the end we find the delicate lyric "Samantha Clara Layton," and another birth, equally joyful. The former poem, however, begins with "and." *And?*

Like Pound's *Cantos*, this century's exemplary epic of the poet in time, Layton's reorganized oeuvre begins with a connective. "And" connects the past, launches the present, projects a future. "And" also joins with the end of the poem, so that the last lines "while someone from afar off/ blows birthday candles for the world" swing back to the beginning to "...me happiest when I compose poems." The last work in *A Wild Peculiar Joy* is "The Wheel," where the poet prepares ("once again") for "the next relentless turn of the wheel," which is fate, the inevitability of tragic creation. Cycles, circles; recurrence; contraries. And: the career begins *in medias res*, as good epics do. This is a personal epic, though, and the hero is the poet (a.k.a. Layton).

"The Birth of Tragedy" provides the impetus for this career: it is a manifesto, a declaration of faith in poetry: "I am their mouth; as a mouth I serve." The next poem, "The Swimmer," is the dive into contemporary currents ("see"). Then the poems echo, contrast, reflect, and enlarge on each other: "The Swimmer," "The Shark," and "The Breaststroke"; "The Birth of Tragedy," "Whatever Else Poetry is Freedom," and "New Tables" and "Sunflowers" (on Marx, he writes: "I think of the young Marx/ heaven-storming Promethean..."); "After Auschwitz" and "Recipe for a Long and Happy Life"; "Absence" and "The Silence"; "Night Music" and "Eine Kleine Nachtmusik"; "For Maxie" and "For my sons, Max and David." Symbols recur: wheels, the Holocaust; dying animals: squirrels, butterflies, cats; martyred poets. Favourite figures: Marx, Nietzsche, Shakespeare, Spinoza, Byron. Criminals, devils and enemies: Stalin, Hitler, materialism, Xians (false believers). Places: Canada, Italy, Israel, Germany, Greece. "And" sex: lovers to inspire and then nag at the poet. In the later poems the tone modulates to disappointment. The message has not penetrated "the bark of complacency and egotism"; we find bitter shock in "For my Neighbours in Hell,"

"The Garden," and "When Hourly I Praised." The poet still lectures the world; but the "I" is less infused with "*Übermenschliche Freude.*"

The contraries in this dialectic are sex (vitality) and death (destruction of the living spirit). Accordingly everything is scaled to two sizes: huge and small. Villains are viewed through the enlarged spactacle of "the improved binoculars": they become swollen giants out of an apocalyptic vision. Animals, plants, and lovers are seen from the reversed perspective: they are vulnerable creatures in need of divine protection. Layton's dialectic is a moral empirical one which finds its synthesis in the first-person singular: the "Unwavering I," the witness and participant, making poetry and his world now. *A Wild Peculiar Joy* consciously bares the route Layton has travelled since 1946.

IV

Unfortunately, "the war of liberation" destroyed his prose. The weakest poems can be included as part of the missionary process, and *Engagements* (1972) and *Taking Sides* (1977) are intended as footnotes to the critical drive of the poetry. The targets are still the anti-life forces; but Layton prefers harangues to discourse. He is now writing his memoirs, which could prove to be a different experience; although given his penchant for Wagnerian dramaturgy, I doubt that it will be.

Consequently, reading *Engagements* is impossible to do. Rants start: "I worship the Divine in extraordinary man, know that all flesh is grass, and that everything ripens into decay and oblivion. Ever since boyhood the pathos of cenotaphs, solemn memorials, and the humbler inscriptions on obscure tombstones has always moved me to tears. The poetry is in the pathos. The genitals of a Casanova, the brain cells of an Einstein — the eternal flux atomizes them with the same grand indifference... Laughter-provoking therefore apear to me all Christian revivalisms (whether of the Eliotic and Billy Graham stripe), rabid nationalism, civic respectability, psychoanalysis — those pitiful dodged of the aging, the weak-kneed and hysterical" (*Engagements*, p. 81). Sixty-seven pages later, in a Foreword written twelve years after the one quoted above, the tantrum continues: "Yahoos, sex-drained executives, pimps and poetasters, limping critics, graceless sluts and the few, the rare few, who gave me moments of insight or ecstasy: I am crazy enough to think I have given them immortality." (p. 148) And goes on: "This is too much! When several months ago a hyperthyroidal female with a side interest in my sexual virility wrote a dishonest account... of the views I had expressed at the Canadian Arts Conference, I let it pass. After all I can't spend all of my life enlightening people, shaking the quirks and crotchets out of them..." (p. 170).

Layton regards himself as an aphorist, and certainly a collection like *The Whole Bloody Bird* (1969) succeeds as a demonstration of mixed modes. But the aphorism explodes prose. It is suited to the polemic and few aphorists can employ a prose line shaped to the sequential development of an argument. Layton's identification with the manner of Nietzsche's scandalous icono-clasm (I believe he always thought that Nietzsche was Jewish) turned his own prose into melodramatic Sturm und Drang, a grotesque parody of his Raging Bull image. Moments of lively wit do appear in the aphorisms in *Taking Sides* (pp. 219-222) and in his "Introductory Note to Canadian Poems, 1850-1952," where his sense of humour has a quick puncturing impact.

When Layton's Forewords are read in the volumes for which they were intended, their context is more obvious. Written in the ruthless irreverent style of Shaw's Prefaces to *Man and Superman* and *Saint Joan*, these missiles sometimes find their targets, like Wasps, "Xians," Northrop Frye's school of Myth Criticism, and Canadian complacency. From the Foreword to *The Covenant* (1977):

> The alert and sensitive poet seizes the moment of significant change when old values and institutions are crumbling into hypocrisy and cowardice and new impulses are beginning to reveal themselves... Still, nothing finally endures except truth, and laughter is mankind's best purgative... If noxious or foolish doctrines can never be refuted, perhaps they can be laughed to death.... (pp. xiv-xv)

A blast that echoes *ridende dicere severum*, the epigraph to Nietzsche's "The Case of Wagner."

Strangely, the problem in the essays and Forewords is with the voice. The lover, the clown, the prophet and the hero, are dramatic masks. They are personae which support the Larger-than-Life rhetoric. But in the Prefaces and Introductions, the high and the low style (the hero and the fool) cancel each other out. The incisive qualities of his poetry disintegrate, and you receive an impression of dogmatic power, a rage smashing out of the ghosts haunting Layton's mind. Violent reaction melts into comedy. The Carlyle-like tone collides with the practical schoolteacher. Intuitions become simplified pontifications: "I am a genius who has written poems that will survive with the best of Shakespeare, Wordsworth, and Keats..." (*Engagements*, p. 169). And: "The French are a cold, egocentric, logical people: long ago love was murdered there" (p. 101). And: "Looked at with the cold eye of psychoanalysis, Christianity can be viewed as a severe neurosis whose consequences — self-hatred, hubris, guilt, and intolerance may explain the horrendous sadistic cruelties which Europeans with the blessing of popes, bishops, and priests have inflicted on the Jews..." (*For My Brother Jesus*, 1976, p. xvii). And: "Man is a diseased animal, spoke Nietzsche, spoke Freud. Of course he is. Blame his malaise on sexual repression...." (*Engagements*, p. 89). His film and literary reviews have more insight: the letters on "Fellini's Casanova" and "Last Tango in Paris" in *Taking Sides*, and the analysis of *Othello* in *The Whole Bloody Bird* are observant discussions of symbols and names. Yet even in a lecture like "Prince Hamlet and the Beatniks," which stresses the importance of the artist's involvement in history despite his idealistic inclinations toward "love and meditation," we find that ceremonial nineteenth-century rhetoric. Layton's clumsiness deflects attention from the content of his pronouncements. Indeed, his prose generally shows this concern for the message over the craft. The short stories assembled in *Engagements* reveal a good eye for detail and ear for inflection and slang, a talent he never pursued.

Perhaps Layton's poetic persona could never adapt to the paces of prose. Perhaps the lack of debate in Canadian literary circles inspired nothing more than impudent filibusters and impatient lectures. But the experience of reading his prose is painful, once you recall the power of his poetry. And what is unexpected is the apparent cause for this "reactionary" prose manner: the estrangement which hides behind Layton's shouts, the feeling that his historical urgency was being shunted aside by a culture of hockey pucks, beer bottles, and survival in the bush. For *Engagements* suggest the image of someone making a frantic effort to spark a "culture of crisis,"[17] someplace where he could feel at home, as though the book were a collage of lonely appeals bellowed from that shakily constructed prophet's tower.

*   *   *

He who cannot take sides should keep silent.

Genuine polemics approach a book as lovingly as a
cannibal spices a baby.

The virility of works lies in assault.

The destructive character knows only one watchword:
make room: only one activity: clearing away.

The destructive character is young and cheerful.

Although these quotations could (again) be from a Layton
polemic, they are from Walter Benjamin's *One Way Street and other
Writings*.[18] Benjamin — a German Jew who committed suicide
rather than be taken prisoner by the Nazis — was a student of Karl
Kraus, a Marxist, a friend of Brecht's, an aphorist and iconoclast
at home in Baudelaire's Paris. He wrote no poetry (that I am
aware of) and there is no direct line of influence. It is the context of
combat that is important, of revolutionary polemics and language
as a lash. This is the tradition of The Word which animates the
work of Heine, Kraus, and the Jewish humanists in our day, Elias
Canetti and George Steiner. The destructive character in
Benjamin's sense, is always engaged in clearing away, and
Layton, with his usual comic braggadocio, has declared: "I
liberated the constipated spirit of Canadians. They think of me
when they make love"; and: "Anglo-Saxon man is riveted by
religion and sex and sin. He thinks of sex as so much wasted
energy..." (*Taking Sides*, p. 222). Layton was one of the first
Canadian writers to incorporate explicit sexual language into his
work. Again he cut a seemingly lonely route, although he was
operating in the Lawrence-Miller-Mailer-Burroughs line of
visceral emphasis; nor did he suffer the hounding censorship that
D.H. Lawrence endured. It has been Margaret Laurence (of all
people) who has provoked the fury of our Puritans. Like D.H.
Lawrence, Layton is a celebrant of sex who seeks revelation in "a
woman's pudend." He is *a sex evangelist*.

Certainly, Layton was preaching about physical joy before
sexual freedom became a past-time of adolescents, secretaries,
journalists, politicians, and professors. He has, however, (with a
shocking lack of attention) continued to mock middle-class
morality and sexual prudishness to an audience that grew up with
Pierre Trudeau, Viet-Nam, rock'n'roll, abortion and the pill.

In *Engagements* and *Taking Sides* the second-handedness of
Layton's perceptions makes his orations sound like a jumble of

Marx, Nietzsche, D.H. Lawrence, and Solzhenitsyn. But Layton wanted to be a great man, not a great writer. His uniqueness is that he announced these things in a nation "whose intellectual history skipped out what happened in Europe after the middle of the eighteenth-century," as Hugh Hood has said. Layton felt it was his fate to fuse the Romantic-Rebel with classical verse forms, a messianic message with political debate, the lament with dissent, "divine sarcasm" with the tragic mask. Yet "what can I know?" the aging voice asks after the long battle in "Nominalist," a touching "final" meditation in *A Wild Peculiar Joy*. He answers, *sotto voce*:

> The tremulous black-coated squirrel
> all instinct and fear
> unique as the tree's bark....
>
> My own storm-tossed soul,
> a troubling joy
> since the day I was born....

V

Layton's poems and polemics thus should be read as an apologia for the poet as a freedom fighter. In *A Wild Peculiar Joy* and *The Collected Poems*, the poet damns his diminishing position as a secretary to the pressures of place, the impositions of time. For if there are no received routes in the new land and the modern audience is losing its feel for poetry, then the poet must engage these facts and demand attention. If the artist is surrounded by billboards, captions and commercials (all of them "authorless"), then he must load his words with individuality so that we can read his book and say *this* writing has character. Layton's attacks on super-critics like Frye, and his fury against materialism, stem from this understanding that the poet's visions are being patronized and (worse) abstracted from life. As he writes in the Foreword to *The Gucci Bag*:

> What makes for enduring poetry is the intersection between the personal and the universal: on a lesser scale, between the personal and social. Only a handful of North American poets have essayed anything like that in recent decades. Robert Lowell? John Berryman? Who else? Is there a poet anywhere

in Canada or the United States who is addressing himself with the full force of his talent and personality to the inequities and insanities which our disintegrating bourgeois-bolshevist world is manifesting on all sides? The professors and critics, as I predicted in numerous prefaces, have done their deadly work. More at home with ideas and abstractions than they are with feelings and experiences, their influence has been such as to practically eliminate personality from contemporary poetry. It's almost impossible in the welter of anonymous voices to distinguish one poetaster from another. (p. 3)

The problem with Layton's unified effort is, and has always been, that *his understanding of the mad-prophet is theoretical*. He is one of the least deranged or irrational poets of his time. His desires are generally rooted humane ones, as even his sarcastic poems show. You need only compare his rants to Artaud's, to Pound's Rome radio speeches, or compare his career to Robert Lowell's or John Berryman's (one: mad; the other: a suicide), to recognize the difference. The point is moot. Layton emphasized his prophetic vocation to the extent that it marred his talent as Canada's premier poetic witness. He surely understands the dehumanization of modern society and he has raged against those writers who have betrayed their humanity to the assembly of the faceless. Layton's *intellectual* understanding of the Canadian cultural milieu told him that what was needed was a Swift, a Nietzsche. He may have been right; but he is himself too in love with life (and women), too tough, too much a man of the world and too much of a teacher, to have fully followed that "god-damned" line. "I always know exactly what I'm doing and why," he has said. This is why his prose strikes false notes. It is why his poetry yields to self-parody. It is why he has peculiar blind-spots in his vision. It is also why it was inevitable for this poet-critic to become caught in the rigid direction of his fight. Once he forged his "mad role" he was locked into it, and the "eternal rebel" became the "Acceptable Variant." Yet the late poems that we find in *The Gucci Bag* and other volumes, his voice continues to be outraged on a huge scale. Which is why he has referred to other poets as Lesser-than-Life. Heroes are *supposed* to be elemental figures, and the voice of the liberated individual must go on sounding maddened by the (inevitable) lack of Superman contact.

Still, there is a desperate undercurrent in those poems written after 1980. This comes from the estrangement most writers feel when their concerns oppose the values of a commercial society. Alienated artists often deliberately make enemies because if you have an enemy then you at least have someone you can talk to. (Layton has felt this way about Northrop Frye.) Layton had a nose for the garbage in Canada and he fought hard to create a context for other poets. And through his grand gestures, he has clarified some of the choices available for late twentieth-century writers: if you make your life the ground of your writings, the result is either self-destruction or mythomania. Few writers have been as generous as Layton. Yet his confinement in his "mission" has been tight. This is another reason why his prose has been a failure, for prose requires a flexible patience that extends over pages, and ultimately for all Layton's identification with voices like Heine's and Yeats', there is only that determined *one*: the poet as temporal tourist, the poet as monument.

Part of our dilemma as critics is to separate symptom from diagnosis: who personifies the epoch's problems and who is exposing them with scalpel and light. You can perform diagnosis and surgery on your own symptoms, make yourself the operating room and then poke, prod, make incisions and amputations. Norman Mailer, a writer to whom Layton is frequently compared, is such a diagnostician. It is unfair to compare a poet with a prose writer; but the extreme contrast should help us to see the issue. Mailer's meditations in *Advertisements for Myself* (1959), *Cannibals and Christians* (1966), *Existential Errands* (1972), and *Pieces and Pontifications* (1982), are mosaic minefields of discoveries. His self-aggrandizing antics have deflected attention from his ethical concerns: the integrity of the self under existential pressure, the imagination's link with past, present and future, the impact of technological change on language and sexuality. Both Layton and Mailer are democratic writers who vulgarize their style to reach a large readership. Both are infused with the demon and the dark. The difference is in method, temperament and audience: Mailer's ground is novelistic, reportorial, located in consuming America; Layton's is poetic, didactic, located in cautious Canada. Mailer developed radical mobility because he researched the fluctuations of the age. Layton has moved physically, but in the strategies of his rhetoric, he has remained remarkably still. Like many Canadian writers, Layton's view of the world is fixed in the nineteenth century. His dream of a humane synthesis is a fine thing to advocate, but Mailer, perhaps inadvertently, and more terrifyingly, has *shown* the bankruptcy of the secular faiths in North American society. Layton's reaction was to continually "howl" and "weep".

It is perhaps pointless to speculate on how a writer's career might have developed had he matured in a more literate environment. The matrix of writer-reader-publisher-editor-critic is a combination which cannot be predicted in any sociological way. Yet "we are the children of our landscape" Lawrence Durrell writes. History throws up figures: words call, and the artist launches his journey. But when a whole culture struggles toward voice, heaving itself out of the anonymous and the borrowed, certain authors are thrust forward to become *autho*rities. The value of Layton's work is that he made himself and his poems integral to our imaginations. However, the Canadian literary scene did not offer the understanding Layton needed. So he had to steel himself. "There's nothing any critic can tell me about myself" he declared. But to keep writing Layton had to become more and more personally identified with his poetry, so that the autobiographical reference is necessary for our reading. Thus the prose falls to the wayside. There are no more short stories. His letters sound like discarded shards from the poetry. His occasional book reviews come alive only when he writes about someone who seems like himself. *The voice* is assured only when angered and overwhelmed by that which it has always been touched and troubled by.

Although Layton rejected exile, he had, I believe, a sense that there would be a cost for his staying in static Canada. His best poems, "The Bull Calf," "The Birth of Tragedy," "The Shark," "The Predator," and "The Improved Binoculars," contain premonitions, warnings. Which may be why violence and vaudeville lurk under the surface of these poems. Layton believed in his fate; he never questioned himself; he was "caught up." So every attempt to record his experiences has been a counterattack against "blind cages". As he writes of his culture in "From Colony to Nation":

A dull people
but the rivers of this country
are wide and beautiful...

A dull people, without charm
or ideas...

These sentiments are expressed again (and again) in "Centennial Ode" (sometimes called "Confederation Ode"), "Osip Mandel-stam (1881-1940)," "Speculators," "Dialogue," "Baudelaire in a Summer Cottage," and "Ah, Nuts." Pick up *any* volume or interview he has published since *Here and Now*: there will be one poem or remark devoted to the subject. The dullness he detested at last had its dulling effect. Layton's lack of self-criticism can be seen when he says in *An Unlikely Affair* (1980), a selection of correspondence with Dorothy Rath, that:

> I've never had any doubt about its [his poetry's] permanent value, and all that has happened in the past decade or so is that at last other people are coming around to my way of thinking. My work... has made its way into the minds and hearts of my countrymen with little or no assistance from anyone... Intellectually Canada was a wasteland when I first began to take myself seriously as a writer and my own feelings and intuitions found little or no support in the cultural atmosphere I was compelled to live in... (pp. 203-204).

The unlikely affair in the title is between this self-proclaimed prophet and his frequently bewildered readers. These letters, worthless as literature, indicate our permanent problem with Layton: they show how self-parody and banality and bluster can exist side by side with grace and humour and perceptiveness.

Thus Layton's failure is that he never reconciled the tension between the demands of craft and his desire to change his world. But then how many have? Greater writers have foundered on those rocks. It may be that his original availability left him open to the elements that could harm his talent. However, it may be that this ultimately destructive vulnerability is the only process which *can* bring insight today. More damaging: Layton's ideology of joy prevented him from transcending the influence of his favourite "Prometheans," Marx and Nietzsche. He remains a poor judge of his work, a man of this age and yet an anachronism, "a realistic idealist" who sought a messianic-heroic role in a time and place that may no longer have a use for that ambition.

Yet when you survey Layton's career, his gift is that he never broke faith with life: he never knuckled under to the steamroller of frigid indifference in Canada; his concerns were never provincial; he never gave in to the abyss that murdered others who elected to be "tight-rope dancers." "Black cloud, do not leave me now," Elias Canetti wrote for all writers who choose to swim in history's currents, "Remain over me so that my old age does not go stale, remain inside me, poison of grief, so that I shall not forget the dying." And for those who cannot turn their back, who reject post-modernist "irrealism" and seek the charge of reality, Layton's gift cannot be underestimated.

(1983)

Leonard Cohen:
The Endless Confessions
of a Lady's Man

If the essence of each generation is a particular type of sensibility, an organic capacity for certain deeply-rooted directions of thought, this means that each generation has its special vocation, its historical mission.... But generations, like individuals, sometimes fail in their vocation and leave their mission unachieved.
Ortega Y Gasset

Could give no response in words — his body melted from within — crumpled cloth flapping wind —
William Burroughs

The poet stares from the black and white photographs on the covers of his records and books. His face is dark, handsome, resembling at times Dustin Hoffman in "The Graduate" and Al Pacino in "The Godfather, Part Two." He glares, a haunted look in his eyes, brooding, melancholic, intense. You look again and the photographs from different stages in his career, from *Beautiful Losers* to *The Energy of Slaves*, show increasing *angst*, an emptiness in his eyes. "Le Poète Maudit," the Beat, the Desolate Angel.

Another book, sparsely written, with no photographs of the author, purports to confess about "My Life in Art" and the death of a lady's man. The cover has a Renaissance drawing of a male angel making love to a female angel; the book flap hints of alchemy and "spirituum." Sex, God — or devils? — and death. Surely some revelation is at hand.

The poet's identity is of course Leonard Cohen, novelist, musician, performer, television producer, decadent, dandy, and self-admitted professional liar. Each cover shot reveals the face of a mood, the distinctive pose of a romantic poet.

Romantic! Open to any page of Cohen's *Selected Poems, 1956-1968* and the clean lines will drip over you like lyrical honey:

> Go by oceans,
> Where whales sail,
> Oceans, love,
> I will not fail.[1]

Such natural music. It is like a Renaissance love song or a lyric by *fin-de-siècle* poet, Ernest Dowson. Never mind that Cohen's images often dissolve in the imagination, leaving no trace. Never mind the self-disgusted tone that seeps through his later books. The power of Cohen's work is not found in his writing anyway, but in the uncanny magic of his Public Relations: his image and voice.

Like most true modern Romantics, Leonard Cohen's main mode of expression is the confession. Every work achieves whatever unity it has from one source: himself. His career has been a series of public happenings. Irving Layton lives mythically, historically, self-consciously aware of his joining of the "Egotistical Sublime" with classical satire and American "vers libre." Cohen attempts something similar, but with a sensibility and an intention that are radically different. The troubador of St. Catherine's Street lives in and for the moment: he is a poet of amoral "airs," a Black Romantic "Ariel."

Where Cohen poses an elusive problem is as a *literary* man. In the 1960s, Cohen proceeded from the intuition that the place poetry and fiction had occupied in society had changed. "I never really considered myself a poet," he said, "a poet is something that is dead." Where are the audiences? he asked: listening to records and radios, watching TV, glancing through *Time* magazine, and lining up for movies and concerts. ("Audience": from the Latin "audire," meaning "to hear.") With unerring instinct, he then transformed himself from a poet-novelist into a folk-pop singer. If you want to stay alive, he implied, follow me. Few did, and fewer understood. When in a short time Cohen's popularity was rated by pop magazines as second only to Bob Dylan's, his astonishing success sent tremors through the staid Canadian clubs. As Louis Dudek — a former teacher of Cohen's — declared in a common remark:

> In the resulting confusion, popular entertainers are claimed to be artists of serious value, like the Beatles or Bob Dylan. And genuine artists of promise descend perforce to mere entertainment and become idols or celebrities, like Leonard Cohen who was a fine poet before he "gave that all up"...[2]

Note the past-tense reference to Cohen's talent and the sneer in "mere entertainment."

It is too easy to forget that Cohen recognized that the electronic age offered the possibility of a revival of what Nietzsche called the "folk lyrist"[3]: the aural-oral performance of the musical poet. Cohen's Jewish cool, combined with his rare ability to express tenderness and disorder, was able to reach those who would not normally have read a book of poems. I can attest to the effectiveness of his move because I came to his work through haunting songs like "Suzanne." I knew that he had published several books, but these I lumped with John Lennon's *In His Own Write* and Bob Dylan's odd Beat book, *Tarantula*. Like others, I did not consider Cohen a writer at all until later when I read *Beautiful Losers*.

It has, however, been some time since the Cohen craze. His last major album was "Death of a Lady's Man," overproduced by wall of sound expert Phil Spector; his last important book was ... what? ... a satirical collage? ... prose poem? ... fractured autobiography? ... called *Death of a Lady's Man*. He does not often perform in public these days. Yet despite Cohen's current (non-) status, he has tried to be "absolutely modern"; he is an integral part of a generation's desires. Thus he presents a disturbing case for those who wish to be both attuned to and critics of their age.

Still, re-reading his *Selected Poems* is not always an invigorating experience. There are poems which are so slight they barely exist on the page, like "Owning Everything"; sentimental poems, like "I Met a Woman Long Ago" and "In Almond Trees Lemon Trees"; and terse uneventful lines like "Summer Haiku." Some of Cohen's verse is mild, competent verbiage. He can write with such a graceful style that you hardly notice when nothing is going on. When things go right, Cohen's wit, brevity and suggestive abilities communicate immediate notes:

I heard of a man
who says words so beautifully
that if he only speaks their name
women give themselves to him.

If I am dumb beside your body
while silence blossoms like tumors on our lips
it is because I hear a man climb stairs
and clear his throat outside our door. (p. 30)

"Tumors" twists the lyric toward a dark meaning that will have significance in Cohen's later work. These lines are called, simply, "Poem." In works such as "Summer Night," and "A Kite is a Victim" from what are his best collections, *Let us Compare Mythologies* and *The Spice Box of the Earth*, and a later poem like "I Believe You Heard Your Master Sing," their successful effect is achieved through his remarkably conservative use of rhyme, half-rhymes, unadorned diction, and droning slow rhythm. Poems like the famous "Suzanne Takes You Down" are memorable because they are simply expressed and yet evocative with their religious-mythical imagery, their repetitive beat, and their colloquial diction. In "Last Dance at the Four Penny" and "For Irving Layton" there are hints of Verlaine, touches of Corbière. "What I'm Doing Here" serves as a succinct credo:

I do not know if the world has lied
I have lied
I do not know if the world has conspired against love
I have conspired against love
The atmosphere of torture is no comfort
I have tortured...

Like a nymphomaniac who binds a thousand
into a strange brotherhood
I wait
for each of you to confess[4]

Cohen's stances and strategies are here: the confessional "I," corruption, sex, death, and sentimental ooze. The rhythms and diction are prosaic, repetitive, confident, again incantatory. No extended Whitman-like line; no "Howl"; no complex words appear; nothing arcane. Cohen's diction is plain-man, shaved down to be conveyed quickly.

Yet even his best poems have a delicate vagueness in which no thought or image quite locks together. Cohen's language does not have the earthiness of Layton's or the mythological allusiveness of Octavio Paz's. His poems play on clever remarks, sly poses and dank moods: you have to *feel* what he means, letting the sounds and suggestions slip over you, like a "song" (his most often used title).

However, as Cohen wrote in his first novel, *The Favourite Game*, "Canadians are desperate for a Keats"[5] or desperate for someone who *looks* like a Keats. And *The Favourite Game* (1963) serves as a "self-portrait," a blueprint for Cohen's attempt to capture an audience. An urban novel with powerful descriptive passages about Montreal, *The Favourite Game* is full of contrived self-disclosures and manifestoes, as the poet's surrogate, Lawrence Breavman (a play on bereavement?), is shown to be "double-natured and arbitrary... the persecuted brother... the innocent of the machine toys, the signing judge who listens but does not sentence."[6] The prose is terse, tense, and "poetic"; the form is fragmented, almost epigrammatic. The muses are represented by the invisible presences of Leslie Fiedler and Bob Dylan, and the artist is an actor, a radical innocent who can use the pop tools, while remaining — paradoxically — the only honest man. The book is a "Portrait of the Artist as a Young Con-Man and Don Juan" (the favourite games of the title), as Cohen writes: "The whole enterprise of art was a calculated display of suffering,"[7] and most revealing of all, "The world was being hoaxed by a disciplined melancholy."[8]

The novel ends, abruptly and prophetically, with the apotheosis of a jukebox:

> The jukebox wailed. He believed he understood the longing of the cheap tunes better than anyone there. The Wurlitzer was a great beast, blinking in pain. It was everybody's neon wound. A suffering ventriloquist. It was the kind of pet people wanted. An eternal bear for baiting, with electric blood. Breavman had a quarter to spare. It was fat, it loves its chains, it gobbled and was ready to fester all night. (pp. 222-223)

The last sentence, with its tactically located "fester," again evokes a sinister *taint*. The passage also suggests that if language fails, turn to song. This is a premonition of Cohen's rejection of verbal intelligibility. *The Favourite Game* is stalked by death and disconnection, but it is the clearest statement Cohen has made in his search for a Public Image and for something interesting to say.

Beautiful Losers (1966) represents another "stage," and another sign of his imminent boredom with language and form. "Connect nothing," it shouts (p. 16). "The Plague! It invades my pages of research." (p. 22) The novel is a test of fictional limits, a terminal book, written to "Change! Purify! Experiment! Cauterize! Reverse! Burn! Preserve! Teach!" (p. 175) In this dated 1960s blitz, the plot-line is non-existent, the characters are shadows and mere initials ("F."), historical times mix, voices shriek, physical settings fade in and out, vivid images are dangled before the tantalized reader. The method is the mosaic. Moments startle: the hot-house ambience of a PG rally is established in deft strokes (pp. 117-123); the ranting tone in F.'s long letter has an obsessive audacity (pp. 145-226); the furious fragments devoted to sex, nausea and drugs rival William Burroughs' *Naked Lunch*. However, the vital parts hurtle by, leaving a sense of a breathless blur, a high-flying soft machine which does not ever want to touch ground. Reading this "electrical conversation" is like flipping channels on a radio: the effect is hallucinative, even mesmerizing, and yet somehow inconsequential. Or as Cohen admits with unconscious irony: "This is *the Revenge* of the Radio" (p. 226, emphasis mine).

Again if the fragmentation in *Beautiful Losers* has any point, it is in the working out of the turbulence in Leonard Cohen's mind. And what this divided self is yearning for is *a way out*, a Revelation, "the greatest and truest sacred formula" (p. 130). F. chants hypnotically: "God is alive. Magic is afoot. God is alive. Magic is afoot. God is afoot. Magic is alive. Alive is afoot. Magic never died..." (p. 157). Cohen demands a sexual-spiritual apocalypse, a cosmic confession: "O Father, Nameless and Free of Description, lead me from the Desert of the possible..." (p. 178). *Beautiful Losers* strains toward ecstasy and frenzy; it resembles a huge orgasm. And like anyone who searches for a greater orgasmic "everything," Cohen temporarily finds at the end the ultimate big bang — God. "I will welcome His silence in pain," the spent voice whispers in its final apostrophe.

This search for an apocalyptic *something* (anything?) is essential to Cohen's projection of a Troubled Image. Hence he has inevitably been attracted to the allure of annihiliation, the "charm" of being "nothing." ("Charm": from the old French "charme," meaning enchantment, and the Latin "Carmen," meaning a song, from which comes the Anglo-Saxon "charm," a short poem invoking the supernatural, and the source of the name for Mérimée's and Bizet's seductress "Carmen.") The books and albums Cohen wrote and recorded in the 1970s show the effect of his desire to "connect nothing." Look at *The Energy of Slaves* (1972), a series (suite? cycle?) that falls short of its promise. Here we find intimations of disaster. The poems are mostly untitled, the diction is stark, the rhythms flattened, the vision harsh and candid, the usual Cohen love lyrics filled with unusual desperation. Critics have said that these prose lines are anti-poems, Cohen's attack on himself, even a farewell to art. They can be read as a meditation on the poet's "slavery": his career and confessional posture. He writes: "Each man/ has a way to betray/ the revolution/ This is mine." (p. 122) Then when we arrive at the last lines, beginning with "there is nothing here" (again the ominous pun on "nothing") and ending with "we are naked with our friends" (p. 127), our trouble remains. As brutally bare as this supposed *mea culpa* is, it leaves little behind except for some good lines and a depressed mood, "Une Saison En Enfer" without the technical daring, the passionate perception, the tough satire.

Cohen has made a fetish out of falling short. We have to give him credit: he has broken out of the stolid Canadian milieu, away from the Loyalists and the Back to the Bush Movement, into an international arena where he has "freelanced along the razor's edge." Yet whenever he has returned to something purely literary, the results have been cryptic and sensuous, sometimes alive and allusive, sometimes derivative and obscure, and never approaching an accomplished whole.

Why does this writer remain insubstantial when he is graced with rhythmical suavity and the ability to hypnotize audiences? The answers are unsettling, as they take in what Cohen's public persona has become, and of what his contract with his audience may consist.

It is as if Cohen had to *drain* himself and his words so that he could pour out his image and songs and books to an audience that may, consciously or unconsciously, understand that utter emptiness. *In order to become a "folk-lyrist" he had to become blank.* He is therefore discomforting because he has tuned into the unacknowledged nihilism of our time. This nihilism is not based on an intellectual hopelessness, but on a "tabula rasa" mentality, a mindlessness, a sense of inexplicable loss. We come back to Cohen, hoping for more, hearing something we understand intuitively, fascinated by the anguished mystery he represents. In his later songs and books, Cohen seems to be asking, as if in shock, "How did I get here?" "Why am I confused?" "What went wrong?" And he has become attached to his nihilism, as it gives him a melancholy theme that will resonate with the whirling souls who surround him. His occasional attempts to assume control are undoubtedly sidetracks to what he feels, which is as he has said in interviews "wiped out" ... "in a hole"...

Another reason he has fallen short is his preference for sentiment, sensation and confession over irony, clarity, and thought. Cohen does not apparently want to be trapped in any sort of conscious activity. He has said:

> ... my strength is that I have no ideas. I feel empty. I have never dazzled myself with thought, particularly my own thought...[9]

This is a leg-pull. (Cohen loves to tease his interviewers.) But it carries some truth. Cohen does not seek ideas in things: his images are never that concrete. So to fully respond to his work, you must sink into a sexual, sensual, emotional union with his words, as if his poems were "feather pillows" or some pre-conscious ritual song. Thus Cohen has remained stereotyped as a morose troubador because he is the product of a longing for confession, to wallow in addictions and the ditch, and then to repent and transcend through glib conversion. Cohen's true subject is decay: desolation and night convulse his work; edges blur; voices merge; fragments fire out; objects are presented only to dissolve; nothing is wholly visual or oral; tragedies are hinted at; disintegration and speed feed him; everything is fluid, tumid, and turbulent. He yearns for an apocalypse, a big bang ("Fuck a saint..." he writes in *Beautiful Losers*), and so remains restless, rootless, and dissatisfied ("I feel empty...," he admits), like an eternal teenager infatuated with his own problems. None of this is perhaps for him cause for irony or humour, argument or scrupulous definition. But that he was once called a spokesman for a generation implies an intellectual vacuum, a desperate drift, that may grip his popular audience.

At various points in his life, Cohen has also sought out alternative kinds of intellectual annihilation, from becoming a Zen monk and a Scientologist, to his bizarre attempt to take over "unconditional leadership of the world." Priest, politician, guru, god: each has its obligations and abnegations. Cohen's fine sensitivity would make him peculiarly vulnerable to these callings, and he has written out of his obsessions with the come-on of the decadent aesthete, supposedly with the "honesty" of "a slave." (Yet what is he a slave to? Who are the masters?) But a slave must twist on the end of a leash or else make an effort to escape. Cohen has tried to slip free, and *Death of a Lady's Man* (1978) is, I think, a record of the attempt.

The book is exasperating. Cohen is not strong on coherence, and *Death of a Lady's Man* is no exception. "Only dis-connect" could be its epigraph. Yet, typically, *Death of a Lady's Man* has some powerful passages, so you wonder what it was that he was after.

Like F. Scott Fitzgerald's autobiographical collection, *The Crack-Up*, Cohen's book may offer "the consolations of a diary" (p.

88), a pseudo-treatise on literary style, a dialogue between the poet and his Other (pp. 46-47). It is egocentric to the point of narcissistic preciousness. But by now you must realize that if you are going to read a lot of Cohen, you have to be *extremely* interested in Cohen himself, or at the very least recognize in him a mirror image of your own troubles. The novel (?) mixes modes, poetry and prose, to expose "My Life in Art." It is his most serious work; it is his most trivial. "Beyond a general sense of his dis-ease," he writes, "he never makes clear the actual mechanics of his anxiety" (p. 39). No, Cohen is not clear about what the "dis-ease" is. It may be that *Death of a Lady's Man* contains Cohen's understanding of the mystification of his image that has occurred, the hallucinations and delusions he has worked within. *Death of a Lady's Man* charts a movement toward distance (maybe). It begins with a first-person narrative and ends with a sort of detached first-person analysis of the author, "Leonard." In between, he writes in "The Asthmatic" that: "I have begun to turn against this man and this book" (p. 64).

Then we see, with startling clarity, that Cohen's writing has become *the poetry of solipsism*. The lovers, the voices, the poets, the things, rarely have "otherness." Everything is unreal. The "you" Cohen uses seems to be YOU out there. It is actually Cohen stuck spinning around on himself. The piece entitled "To Deal With You" is a good example. On the left side of the page, we have an address either to the reader or to Cohen's Other, a passage which presses toward revelation about the artist's obsessions:

And now to deal with you. I am glad that you no longer consider yourself "God's exclusive pet..." It was a crude charlatan's trick, trying to associate the obscurity of your style with the mystery of the godhead. This and nothing else is my voice. It is in you. It has caught into you and it is there like sexual desire. (p. 48)

However, this is not really meant for "you" at all — you can never be sure, despite his trim and economical language — because on the other page we find a pseudo-commentary on what we have read. Here, set in italics, is a voice raising the questions that a critical reader (or an Other?) should ask:

A man has set a fishhook in his lip. Does this mean we can believe what he says? Does he think of himself as the catch or the bait? Is anyone bored enough to reel him in? This paragraph is, I believe, an invitation for the truly bored to

come out of the closet and be baffled one more time, one last
time. Those who do not rest forever in a vindicated hostility,
those who can read past the vindication, will discover deep in
the strata of their boredom the fuel of a great activity. The
mouth of the napping critic will be torn away. The
disfiguring yawn of brotherhood will be penetrated.... (p. 49)

Self-analysis? self-disclosure? or just destruction of plain sense? Is
Cohen leaping for the reader's throat, like Baudelaire in the
"Preface" to *Les Fleurs du Mal*? The passage is certainly full of
"ennui."

In the "Final Examination" (and perhaps *Death of a Lady's
Man* is meant as an anatomy lesson, a hospital, a recovery ward), a
cool voice talks of "Leonard... hobbling with his love" (p. 212). "*I
have examined the heart,*" he claims. The heart of what? Cohen
himself? our electronic times? the individual and history? the
heart... of darkness? The confessional mode is again confirmed: "*I
swear to the police that I have appeared, and do appear, as one of the voices.*"
New directions are hinted at: his death belongs to the future.
However, Cohen is alive, as we know. The death alluded to is
perhaps of the author Cohen. If everything has been rendered
unreal, then the one remaining reality is death, or a spiritual-
intellectual death of some sort. So no more Orpheus among the
damned, ready and willing to be ripped apart.

Or that is how it seems. But what we are left with at the end of
the work is... not much. It seems like a diffident parody of a book
("a poet is something that is dead..."). And Cohen has not
produced anything which indicates that he has moved on to a new
stage. Rather than acting as an enigmatic exorcism, *Death of a
Lady's Man* leaves him locked into his solipsism, his minimal-cum-
nihilism. We should not balk at "nihilist." Most modernist writers
live with this is one way or another. Irving Howe writes: "Nihilism
lies at the centre of all that we mean by modernist literature, both
as subject and symptom, a demon overcome and a demon
victorious."[10] Cohen represents a peculiarly contemporary strain:
"the sentimental-commercialization of nihilism," as if Rod
McKuen and Terry Rowe had collaborated with the shades of
Rimbaud and Céline to produce a hit.

Actually, the truest expression of Cohen's feelings of restless
vacancy cannot be found in *Death of a Lady's Man*, but in a peculiar
poem he wrote as a preface to the *New Poems* of Henry Moscovitch
(1982). Moscovitch is a Montreal poet who has taken a permanent
post in the dead zone. He is an authentic artist of the minimalist

abyss, an expert on claustrophobia ("I was found in an alley/ or in some room/ dead long ago./ No one came to my funeral..."[11]). Cohen's "Stanzas for H.M." are intended as a tribute and yet begin as an awkward imitation of a Restoration ode:

> O perfect gentleman, and champion
> of the Royal Throne; O unbroken stone
> of Sinai's heart; I hero of Verdun;
> our greatest poet until now unknown,
> whose banner over Death has always flown
> in wilds of poverty and solitude;
> I thank you for the years you spent alone
> with nothing to hang on to but a mood
> of Glory, searching words that Love could not elude....

Stanzas are stances, a station from which a point of view can be taken. In the poem's latter part, Cohen's voice jarringly drops to a contemporary tone:

> Dear Henry, I know you will forgive these
> lines of mine, their clumsy antique tone,
> for they are true and not mere obsequies,
> and for all their rhetoric overblown
> a simple gesture to the man you own,
> whose friendship is so rare, whose art so pure,
> simplicity is dazed, then overthrown —
> alarmed and shy my love must I obscure
> behind the fallen grandiose of literature.

Finally, the pathetic admission:

> I don't know where I'm going anymore.
> I find myself a table and a chair.
> I wait, I don't know what I'm waiting for.
> I change the room, the country. I compare
> my clattering armoured blitz to your spare
> weaponry of light, your refined address —
> I know you stand where none of us would dare,
> I know you kneel where none of us would guess,
> well-ordered and alone, huge heart, self-pitiless.[12]

As with *Death of a Lady's Man*, we are once more invited to witness the "revelation" of the poet's paralysis. He seems incapable of daring to find a way out of his *packaging*. And here he has confessed everything he has left, which is (literally) nil.

You have now seen how easy it is to condemn Leonard Cohen. However, *Death of a Lady's Man* does leave some promise that he may break free from his inwardness, his Romantic Agony, his refusal to use words as though they had referential meaning; and interestingly, other than "Stanzas for H.M." and rumours of work on a new book, he has been almost silent since he wrote it. Cohen has done a superb job of marketing himself and of making us believe that there may yet be *something* to his "magic" mutterings.

But I'm still left with suspicions about this... seduction. I wonder why we hold out hope for Cohen, why we applaud his misfortune and his self-abuse, avidly listening when he chants "Take my dignity/ Take my fame/ Take my style/ Take my honour/ Take my courage/ Take my time... I can't stand who I am" (from "Don't Pass Me By" on the "Live Songs" album), and yet we are unwilling to grant him the final authority of a master. This may be because, as *Death of a Lady's Man* reveals, Cohen has "charm," he is available, he is bored, and *he no longer cares about what he says*. Cohen uses the "I" in his writings, but he may not have an "I" to express. Like a transplanted character from Samuel Beckett's *Molloy, Malone Dies*, and *The Unnamable*, Cohen has his "nothing" to say and he keeps saying it, in reduced appearances, as singer-songwriter, former poet and novelist, as film-maker and actor, creating variations on a vision of love turned nightmare that he stopped experiencing and now remembers dimly in confused and yet cleverly constructed bits. That numb, narrowed position is probably appropriate for one of the children of modernism. There are times when Cohen has had glimpses of his entanglement in a celebrity bad faith, as when he writes to a fellow poet in *The Energy of Slaves*:

> Welcome to this book of slaves
> which I wrote during your exile
> you lucky son-of-a-bitch
> while I had to contend
> with all the flabby liars
> of the Aquarian Age[13]

"The flabby liars of the Aquarian Age" are those like Cohen and those who listened to him without acknowledging the compulsions he felt and sometimes fought.

A final word: could Cohen develop a passion for renewal? More to the point: could he become an indispensible witness if he made an ironic tension out of the self-infatuation in *Death of a Lady's Man*? Forgive my tentative tone. I wouldn't ask these questions if it were not for the fact that when Cohen writes with character and style, as in his best songs, the lyrics of *The Spice-Box of the Earth*, and parts of *Beautiful Losers*, none of his contemporaries can approach him. Really, he writes as if the age itself *has* branded and then battered his talent into heaps and pieces of songs and images. *Il faut être absolument moderne*, Rimbaud announces in a famous phrase at the end of his "season in hell," and those words were and are at once a command, a recognition, and an abdication. So we can read Cohen's poems and novels and listen to his records and hear and see what is the poignant reminder of the dissolution of spirit and mind in our time, the inability of our generation to come to grips with the contract between the word and the world. "And wasn't it a long way down?" Cohen once mourned. Yes, "the age demanded an image" not only of its "accelerated grimace," but of its ravages and ghosts. Cohen's is a *symptomatic* voice of the present, and that voice has seldom begun so elegantly lyrical, only to end so empty and ephemeral.

(1983)

"Stone Angels":
An Essay on Margaret Laurence

"Go to it and give 'em people," he said gently. *"You've got the feeling for 'em. You know how to make 'em live. Go on and put 'em in."*
Thomas Wolfe

When, generations from now, the historian of our times undertakes to describe the assumptions of our culture, he will surely discover that the word reality *is of central importance in his understanding of us.*
Lionel Trilling

Margaret Laurence is hard to write about. This unfortunate fact has been accomplished through the relentless efforts of those critics who have compared her to Tolstoy and George Eliot while trying to treat her work as a model for fictional realism. If the critics have made criticism difficult, Laurence's readers have made it almost impossible. They inevitably burble on about her gutsiness and decency and understanding. I am not implying that a conspiracy exists, merely that Laurence's place is not so much secure as it is untouchable. Like Margaret Atwood, and others of lesser quality, an orthodoxy surrounds the author of the "Manawaka" novels like a fog that shrouds the facts. Laurence has been enshrined as a novelist who embodies the various Canadian Themes of The Small Town, The Land, Survival, and The Internalized Self.

I share some of these feelings for her novels. Laurence is a novelist capable of vivid characterizations and emotional intensity. *The Diviners, A Jest of God, A Bird in the House,* and, best of all, *The Stone Angel* offer earnest portraits of people. When Laurence tunes in to the right characters, like Hagar Shipley and Rachel Cameron, her sense of voice never goes wrong. Yet for all her ability as an "ear-witness," the fictional world we find in her writings is often dull, dour, repetitive, and clumsily constructed. Laurence is not a demanding writer: she has never written anything with an intricate plot; her use of language and form rarely commands the reader to be alert; her mind does not seem comfortable with ideas; the range of her knowledge about human affairs is surprisingly parochial; a great deal of modern life has apparently slipped by her attention. Her story-lines, particularly in *The Stone Angel* and *The Diviners*, always travel along the same routes: they chart what could be called "life-lines," or the growing consciousness of what it means to be merely human in our "age of extremes."

"Merely human".... I do not mean to sound scornful. To be human — or should I say humane? — is no small achievement today (if it ever was). Humanity is going out of style, and to be a definite part of reality for many is... well, undesirable. Conscious mind, the struggle with history, honest emotions, and the scrupulous exploration and criticism of empirical fact do not come easy for our novelists. To her credit, Margaret Laurence has resisted the movements of the moment. She has made communication and compassion her personal crusade: her novels have consistently upheld a humane view of how people can and do live.

Yet what are we to make of a writer whose critics have placed her virtually beyond criticism? Do they deal with the limitations of Laurence's vision? I have been re-reading her works recently, trying to understand the position of affection that she occupies in Canadian writing. My readings brought out things I had not expected.

Her first novel, *This Side Jordan* (1960), is not about Canada. In a conventional and florid manner, this novel describes a transition of power between nations, between England, the colonizer, and Africa, the colony. Laurence writes as an expatriate about a society under the political and social domination of another. The unstated analogies to the Canadian situation (analogies which are suggested by Laurence's later work) are obvious. However, *This Side Jordan* is a first novel, and like most first novels it should be forgiven and forgotten; it wouldn't be in print if it were not for *A Jest of God*. Still, *This Side Jordan*, and the vastly superior collection of short stories called *The Tomorrow-Tamer*, are interesting as points of comparison with the "Manawaka" books.

The story revolves around the troubles of a black school teacher and an English businessman, and their wives. There are monologues that refer to African mythology and poetry, the Bible and British colonial guilt. There is a lot of *talk* about sexual tension. However, *This Side Jordan* is a polished work, and the opening scenes which describe the "high-life" and the descriptions of village life are impressive in themselves. Unfortunately, the novel's optimistic ending about reconciled blacks and whites seems like quaint wishful-liberal thinking, given our knowledge of South Africa and Zimbabwe. V.S. Naipaul she is not. The book's concerns stand out clearly: people and communication. In what could have been called her *A Passage to Africa*, Laurence is hopeful; she is intent on exploring the understanding, or the misunderstandings, that occur between sexes, races, classes, and religions.

If *This Side Jordan* gives little indication of what is to come, then *The Tomorrow-Tamer*, published in 1963, is another matter altogether. Here Laurence's prose has been tempered, the narrative rhythms are quicker, the creation of character and locale are suggestive. "The Rain Child" uses first person narrative with prophetic confidence, and "The Voices of Adamo" is well crafted. *The Prophet's Camel Bell*, also 1963 (an *annum mirabilis* for Laurence), is both a travel-book and exploration of an alien cultural climate, written in the same lyrical style as *This Side Jordan*.

One of the most revealing stories in *The Tomorrow-Tamer* is "Godman's Master." The tale is of a dwarf oracle named Godman Pira who longs for freedom but resist reality. Godman is cast out by his liberator Moses (Laurence is not above using obviously allegorical names), who had been for a time Godman's master. The dwarf disappears and eventually becomes a performer in a theatrical troupe, where Moses discovers him years later. After a narration describing Godman's trials, the tale is climaxed by this exchange:

"You have done well," Moses said. "At first I did not see it, but now I see it."
Godman shrugged.
"I have known the worst and the worst and the worst," he said, "and yet I live. I fear and fear, and yet I live."
"No man," Moses said gently, "can do otherwise."
("Godman's Master," *The Tomorrow-Tamer*, p. 159)

"I have known the worst and the worst and the worst... and yet I live...." That is pure Laurence. Her concerns are embodied in this cadenced sentence, with its incantatory Biblical repetitions, and its evocation of suffering and sensitivity and stoical acceptance.

Reading through the African trilogy, however, does not prepare you for the rush of Arctic air that blasts through the first pages of *The Stone Angel* (1964). Suddenly you are aware, as if you have been grabbed by the shoulders and shaken, that you are in the presence of *a writer*. The novel is so cool and assured that it demands to be read:

> ...So much for sad Regina, now forgotten in Manawaka — as I, Hagar, am doubtless forgotten. And yet I always felt she had only herself to blame, for she was a flimsy, gutless creature, bland as egg custard, caring with martyred devotion for an ungrateful fox-voiced mother year in and year out. When Regina died, from some obscure and maidenly disorder, the old disreputable lady rose from sick-smelling sheets and lived, to the despair of her married sons, another full ten years. No need to say God rest *her* soul, for she must be laughing spitefully in hell, while virginal Regina sighs in heaven. (*The Stone Angel*, p. 4)

Here the conventional style fits the speaker and fits the reader into a world (western Canada): here the tough voice is rooted in the ground of a being, Hagar Shipley, the ninety-year old "Holy Terror," with "stubborn ghost" and stubborn speech, "remembering furiously...."

We are soon so involved in this old woman's opinionated view that it may not occur to us that it is *a* view and not *the* view. Her relatives' opinion, like those belonging to Doris, her daughter-in-law, and Marvin, her stolid son, do not penetrate deeply. In *The Stone Angel* Laurence has discovered the technique that will hold her in good stead for the next four books: the isolated point-of-view, or bias, of a character involved in a suggested multiple perspective. Multiple perspective depends on our ability to read through, past and around the narrative voices: a speaker twists and tells a story while a familiar "other" existence continues, which is sometimes only hinted at. All voices become relative. None of this is new after Faulkner or Joyce. What Laurence achieves by exploring *the measures of selfhood* is to make this narrowed range her greatest strength.

Yet is it difficult to say anything about *The Stone Angel* that has not been said and said again, yawn and on: "Moral Vision in *The Stone Angel*," "*The Stone Angel*: Time and Responsibilty," "Pilgrim's Progress: Margaret Laurence and Hagar Shipley." The saturation point may have been reached with a work which does not seem, frankly, to be an inexhaustible source. Still, nothing should detract from this novel's fundamental quality: the intense readability of its compassionate honesty. *The Stone Angel* has a two-part structure: the contemporary sequences which describe the threat of banishment to an old folk's home and Hagar's impending death are "now," the memories are "then." Laurence's stories generally proceed by a juxtaposing of tenses and times. Time is one of her hidden themes: all Laurence's characters are aware of inheritance and potential. The novel unfolds like an extended dramatic monologue, as Laurence's intention is to provide a psychological portrait of Hagar Shipley, a voice that evokes the sense of *being there*, defined, defiant, and humourless. The obvious and derivative image of the stone angel at the book's opening is her symbol. She is a kind of stone, or "cold angel":

> My bed is cold as winter, and now it seems to me that I am lying as the children used to do, on fields of snow, and they would spread their arms and sweep them down to their sides, and when they rose, there would be the outline of an angel with spread wings. The icy whiteness covers me, drifts over me.... (*The Stone Angel*, p. 81)

Even the long death scene at the end (it consumes nearly one-fifth of the novel) depicts this individual's stubbornness and pride. Hagar dies intact, with her memories and indomitability. On the novel's last page, she transforms the comforting "there, there," into a recognition of something beyond selfhood and speech. And there: the book ends the moment she dies; and there: she is, immovable, in print, like stone.

Thus "the living individual on the printed page."[1] Laurence's next book, *A Jest of God* (sometimes titled *Rachel, Rachel* because of the Paul Newman/Joanne Woodward movie) was published in 1964, and it tries to move further into character revelation through eccentric accents. Rachel Cameron at first sounds withdrawn, neurotic. The firm cadences of *The Stone Angel* unexpectedly modulate to a self-pitying tone, looser syntax, and more internal dialogue:

> There. I am doing it again. This must stop. It isn't good for me. Whenever I find myself thinking in a brooding way, I must simply turn it off and think of something else. God forbid that I should turn into an eccentric. This isn't just imagination. I've seen it happen... I don't have to concern myself yet for a while, surely. Thirty-four is still quite young. But now is the time to watch for it. (*A Jest of God*, p. 2)

While the tone is exact, Rachel Cameron is a seemingly less successful characterization than Hagar Shipley. *A Jest of God* is only intermittently powerful, and some portions, like that affair with Nick, are not fully realized at all. Nick is a stick-figure; he never achieves the depth that Rachel does because he remains finally too much of a type. Yet this is partially where the psychological complexity of the novel is concealed. Whatever seems unrealized or vague about the novel can be attributed to Rachel's "unreliable" point-of-view.

Rachel is always *listening*, and *A Jest of God*, is an echo-chamber of innuendoes, lies, rumours, and dubious speculations. She so misinterprets various utterings and events that a comic air often surrounds her stumblings. These doubts have a destructive and a constructive effect: the failure of words initiates an awareness of what can be trusted and said. The most sensational misinterpretation of events occurs in the affair with Nick which forms the novel's centre. Nick is at first a bachelor; then he is married; then it is discovered that he is single. His motivations appear to be callous and manipulative; but what Rachel may salvage from this is a birth. Then in what is the most touching moment in the book, Rachel finds that she is not going to have a baby. Her sadness is a jolt in this age of abortion: Rachel longs for a birth which she hopes will bring a rebirth for her. Rachel comments on this after a monologue on misapprehension: "I don't know whether he [Nick] meant to lie to me or not" (p. 190).

I don't know, Rachel admits. The next chapter describes her decision to move to Vancouver with her mother, though she acknowledges that her reasons for leaving are clouded with uncertainties: "And this, like everything else, is both true and false" (p. 197); and: "The ironies go on" (p. 200). Thus Rachel's vision is (as it always has been) fragmented and fluid. The novel ends, beautifully, with a prayer and a benediction.

The Fire-Dwellers (1969) offers the isolated point-of-view of Stacey MacAindra. First readings indicate a step beyond the techniques of *The Stone Angel* and *A Jest of God*. We seem to be encountering some personalized and Canadianized version of Dos Passos' *USA Trilogy*. *The Fire-Dwellers* represents the virtues and failures of her writings thus far: it has sloppy writing, a clichéd story, characters who are not fully developed, unconvincing plot coincidence, and an intellectual content that exposes a second-rate mind. Yet again, the ambitious form expresses the character of the protagonist. Stacey MacAindra is an "ordinary" person: she is a middle-class woman approaching middle-age. The book is her world. She can only say what she knows. And again Laurence's evocation of a presence is surely sound: "...Stacey, you sure are joyful first thing in the morning. First thing, hell. It's a quarter to nine, and here's me not dressed yet" (p. 3).

As we read, voices shift from third person to first, narratives shift into interior monologues; there are headlines from TV programs, images recalled from Stacey's childhood in Manawaka, monosyllabic dialogues. Paragraphs are arranged with an eye for design and an ear for rhythm. There are "innovations" which derive from Joyce and William Faulkner, minus the erudite virtuosity of the former and the intoxicated poetry of the latter. *The Fire-Dwellers'* form suggests frantic activity, but what is burning within, emotionally and spiritually, is important. Where *The Stone Angel* describes "final things," and *A Jest of God* describes spinsterhood, this novel focusses on the mid-life disorder. It is also the only book Laurence has located mostly in a city (Vancouver), although like many Canadian novelists, she is not an acute observer of urban existence.

Stacey's *angst* seems different from what we have seen in Laurence's work. Still, the chords are there: self, spirit, and speech. *The Fire-Dwellers* is a tableaux, a series of "real" moments describing a few weeks in the life. The last sentence does not imply a resolution, only a skeptical balance: "She [Stacey] feels the city receding as she slides into sleep. Will it return tomorrow?" (p. 308). We know the answer to that: yes, of course. In the last pages, Stacey recognizes the strength she has always had.

On:

> I thought of the accidents that might easily happen to a person... I thought of the dead baby, my sister, who might have been I... I could not really comprehend these things, but I sensed their strangeness, their disarray. I felt that whatever God might love in this world, it was certainly not order. (p. 59)

A new voice: Vanessa MacLeod in *A Bird in the House*. Written over a number of years, the stories in *A Bird in the House* are a suite organized into a novelistic unit, like Joyce's *Dubliners* and Alice Munro's *Lives of Girls and Women*. Unlike Joyce's work, the book is unified by a central speaker, Vanessa MacLeod. The stories recreate the daily mundane and significant events that compose a childhood in western Canada during the depression and the Second World War. The style is graceful and lyrical: it is her most polished and poised work other than *The Stone Angel*. An air of patient love informs this study of a family; life is arduous and confined for Vanessa, but it is not bleak or terrible.

Laurence's realism in these stories is so persuasive that the reader may not be aware of how selective her techniques are. No one character can be wholly sensitive to detail. The author must provide their world. But the interaction of environment (the external) and subjective voice (the internal) is imperative to *the tension* of realism. Selective realism is critical realism. Like all Laurence's works, *A Bird in the House* maps an individual's changes without positing change and the internal as absolutes. That is why her narrative voices are objectified and consistent. Vanessa engages experience and yet remains both in her world and possessed of an inner life which reflects the external. In "Jericho's Brick Battlements" one of Laurence's best stories, the changes which have occurred in the collection are summarized by Vanessa, as the family house she returns to endures like "the stone angel," altered and yet unaltered, a monument to her family's "old indomitability":

> I did not go to look at Grandfather Connor's grave. There was no need. It was not his monument.
>
> I parked the car beside the Brick House... The house had been lived in by strangers for a long time. I had not thought it would hurt me to see it in other hands, but it did. I wanted to tell them to trim their hedges, to repaint the windowframes, to pay heed to repairs. I had feared and fought the old man, yet he proclaimed himself in my veins... ("Jericho's Brick Battlements" *A Bird in the House*, p. 207)

A fine passage that describes the instant of accord and co-suffering with the past, present, and future.

I am suddenly reminded that Laurence's humanist vision has got her into trouble with censors and schoolboards. It is fantastic that the Fundamentalists and Parent Leagues should be up in arms over the physical aspects of her writings (read: sex), because Laurence is something of a sexual clinician. Rachel, Stacey, Vanessa, and Morag in *The Diviners* do not do *it* like rabbits, and she is sturdily non-romantic about The Act itself. *It* is provided as a realistic note. Her characters are happily heterosexual, Calla Mackie in *A Jest of God* notwithstanding. None are miscreants, onanists, or bestial-ists. There is in short little to "bear" in her books. *The Fire-Dwellers* describes sex with restraint, and all her novels are written in sharp contrast to *Quiet Days in Clichy*. However, if there is one thing some readers fear, it is the rendering of what is human. The angry hurt that critical realism provokes cannot be dismissed as an inability to comprehend "imaginative content." Some philistines know their business very well. Their actions can be crushingly successful. An honest writer in a muddled time can be seen as deluded, even sinister. Stendhal, a great pioneer of realism in fiction, wrote in *Scarlet and Black* what is still the best defense of the novel as a portrait and critique of manners, motives, the real life of society:

> Why, my good sir, a novel is a mirror journeying down the high road. Sometimes it reflects to your view the azure blue of heaven, sometimes the mire in the puddles on the road below. And the man who carries the mirror in his pack will be accused by you of being immoral! His mirror reflects the mire, and you blame the mirror! Blame rather the high road on which the puddle lies, and still more the inspector of roads and highways who lets water stand there and the puddle form.[2]

But why write novels today? Who cares about what they show, state, or sing, outside a small band of professional readers? "Indeed why!" Doris Lessing responds in her Preface to *The Golden Notebook* (1962). "I suppose we have to go on living as if...."[3] Lessing answers the question by writing a brilliant six-hundred page novel. The novel is a humane form, and to write a serious one implies understanding can be gained from addressing moral issues. In Canada the audacious novel has been represented by... how many? It is the poem, the short story and the novella which dominate our new "tradition." The short works of Alice Munro, Norman Levine, Mavis Gallant, Barry Callaghan, John Metcalf, and Guy Vanderhaeghe have received more attention than any long novels. Laurence has stuck with traditional fiction, and though her short stories are accomplished, her heart is with what D.H. Lawrence once called "the bright book of life."

Which brings me to *The Diviners* (1974). A big, baggy monster, it is Laurence's "Portrait of the Artist as a Young Woman in Canadian Writing." Like *The Stone Angel*, Morag Gunn is "rampant with memory"; like *The Fire-Dwellers*, there are interior monologues and several narrators; like *A Bird in the House*, the novel explores family roots, love, independence, and creativity. But in *The Diviners* there is a rough, restless quality to the prose which suggests a willingness to try almost *anything*. The form is also vaguely mimetic: the prose rhythms mime the development of Morag's mind and sensibility. Laurence's realism is an expression of her convictions. Thus in her novels this "felt"-intuitive form becomes that which embodies the subject at hand: Hagar requires a spare, sarcastic prose; Rachel's damp yearnings inspire a delicate prose-poetry; Stacey's crisis leads to fractured points-of-view and diminished diction; Vanessa's lyrical reminiscences lead to the gentle autobiographical manner of *A Bird in the House* (and the pseudo-Biblical effusions that pass for interior monologues in *This Side Jordan* lead nowhere at all); and finally the need to embrace as much as possible leads to the flexibility and awkward vulnerability of Morag's point-of-view. *The Diviners* is in fact a review of Laurence's Manawaka world: "All the names. Stacey Cameron. Mavis Duncan. Julie Kazlik. Ross McVitie. Mike Lobodiak. Al Cates. Steve Kowalski. Vanessa MacLeod. Jamie Halpern. Eva Winkler. And so on and so on." (p. 32)

And yet a lot has been left out of her "Portrait of an Artist." We see Morag writing books and dealing with publishers, but none of these experiences are as well described as physical settings, like the Otonabee River. This absence extends to the lack of a political, historical, and intellectual frame, despite Laurence's interest in events like the Riel Rebellion. The possibility of examining the writer in a time of Canadian nationalism could have been exciting. Typically, *The Diviners* abandons background for foreground. Morag never seems concerned with the Writers' Union, the Canada Council, literary magazines, editors, politics, historical events, and international publications, the social *machinery*. Morag is seldom shown reading anybody else either. Who are her influences? Why does she write? Who is she writing for? Her writer lives in isolation, in an internalized world. What Laurence seems to suggest by her image of intense privacy is that what matters is *self*-expression, an oddly nostalgic and Romantic notion for a contemporary writer of near-naturalism.

However, *The Diviners* places a solitary middle-class individual under observation, and it does mostly succeed in articulating the process of an author summing up her crafts and beliefs. "Your writing is your real worth," a character informs Morag, "It's there you have to make your statement." Morag reflects: "Or not make it.... they'd been real to her, the people in her books. Breathing inside her head." (p. 58) In the end Morag remains, like all Laurence's characters, *someone who is largely inadequate to the understanding of the modern world.*

"Whole sight; or all the rest is desolation."[4] So begins one of the most ambitious British novels of the 1970s, John Fowles' *Daniel Martin*, and there is a similar ambition in *The Diviners*. Three years separate the publication of the two books, and I can find no evidence to prove that one author is aware of the other. But compare: *Daniel Martin* and *The Diviners* explore the crisis of the middle-aged artist. In each case, the authors have, by the time of publication, a considerable following among readers and critics. They take risks: the book becomes A Book. First drafts exist beside polished passages; points-of-view sometimes shift within the space of one sentence; time changes occur suddenly. The prose becomes exploratory; the syntax sometimes seems eccentric, undisciplined; there are interpolations of poems, songs, meditations and lists; the form strains toward satire. Fowles and Laurence are intent on examining being now, though as I've said, Laurence's perceptions of our whirling present are not as comprehensive as Fowles'. In *Daniel Martin*, there is an explicit rejection of despair, and this is implicit in Laurence's novel. "To hell with cultural fashion," Fowles writes, "to hell with elitist guilt; to hell with existentialist nausea; and above all, to hell with the imagined that does not say, not only in, but behind the images, the real."[5] Both novels are culminative works which end with a recognition of living tensions, existence in this world. Unlike *Daniel Martin*, though, *The Diviners* seems like an end, and not a beginning, a last chord in her set of voices.

After *The Diviners* comes *Heart of a Stranger* (1976), a collection of previously published articles and autobiographical pieces. There is one good essay, "A Place to Stand On," but Laurence has not developed into a provocative writer of critical prose. Without the voice of a Morag, the Laurentian manner is waffling, sentimental, nice, in the accepted Canadian style.

What, then, can be said about her work? Laurence offers an oeuvre which is arguably the most sympathetically-minded corpus in Canadian fiction. Her women live as full, flawed, often floundering beings; they live humanly, skeptically, without an irritable reaching after abstract faiths and comforting falsehoods; they live with life as they find it: harsh, painful, comical, confounding, and ultimately opaque. Laurence writes:

The theme of survival — not just physical survival, but the preservation of some human dignity and in the end some human warmth and ability to reach out and touch others — this is, I have come to think, an almost inevitable theme for a

writer such as I, who came from a Scots-Irish background...
and who grew up during the drought and depression of the
thirties and then the war. ("A Place to Stand On," from *Heart
of a Stranger*, p. 6).

Her women learn to accept separation and what is separate in
others. Note that the title of Laurence's collection of articles and
travel pieces is *Heart of a Stranger*. But the feeling of being a stranger
is not a failure of will or a dissolution of integrity. Her novels are
populated by people, not demons, heroes, hysterics or ghosts. "I
am the mother now," Rachel says in the last pages of *A Jest of God*.
That is a declaration of human fidelity.

However, their separateness is ambivalent because the speech
her characters rise to is a form of communion. Laurence is, above
all, a spiritual writer, as a glance at her book titles will verify.
Communication becomes the moment of community: the trust in
speech is a faith in sharing and love. So Rachel in *A Jest of God*
searches for communion and comprehension, as the "speaking in
tongues" episode illustrates. The split between what characters
like Hagar and Stacey think and say is a further example. Morag
becomes a diviner, or listener, through the power of the pen,
sounding the depths of her life, and eventually settling on an
acceptance of her world and her work and her family and friends.
The only grace Morag finds is one that is granted through art. We
observe that the title of the novel which Morag is writing is, as it is
hinted in the last lines, *The Diviners*.

Laurence's women, however, are not only seen alone, but
they are seen and heard from the inside, too. The loneliness in her
books was bound to touch a time which knows about inadequacy,
estrangement, divorce. Laurence's characters never seem to be
persuaded that life is truly worthwhile, or even good. Again to her
credit, she does not offer false hopes or easy answers: hers is finally a
lonely, stoical acceptance. Despite the introspective quality of the
Manawaka books, Laurence attends to the world. The self-
awareness of her characters does not depend on the dissolution of
the external or of otherness, nor does it depend on a hatred of life
and the urge to overcome it by creating an internal transcendence.
Her characters edge toward a way of reconciling and being. Thus
Hagar, Rachel, Stacey, Vanessa, and Morag all *remain* like "stone
angels." "Everything is artificial these days," Hagar declares
"...Silks and people have gone out of style, or no one can afford
them any more" (*The Stone Angel*, p. 28). Only at the end of her life
does she understand: "Oh, I am unchangeable, unregenerate. *I go*

on speaking in the same way, always..." (p. 293; emphasis mine).

Now it's time to admit the worst. As mature as these passions of Laurence's are, she can be an astonishingly drab writer. I tended to flip through her works when I re-read them. Moreover, since *The Diviners*, she appears to have backed herself into an artistic corner. I have no idea why this is so. Logically, for a novelist like Laurence, technical experimentation is irrelevant. She could, or should, just go on, "speaking in the same way, always...." It could be that she has listened too hard to the encomiums of the "Can.Cultists," ever eager to box and sell another classic, or it could be that the voices have just stopped (one hopes temporarily). Nevertheless, there is a resolved feeling about her oeuvre, a sense that all further work is likely to be a minor variation on her modest theme.

With customary honesty, Laurence seems conscious of her limited range. "...the kind of novel which I can best handle," she has said, "is one in which the fictional characters are very definitely *themselves*, not me, the kind of novel in which I can feel a deep sense of connection with the main character without a total identification, which for me would prevent a necessary distancing."[6] And: "With my generation, the great thing was the exploration of personality."[7] It is possible that Laurence is more aware than her critics that other than *The Stone Angel*, her novels do not repay close readings. But then not many novels do, or were meant to. She is no Tolstoy, nor is she the author of disguised Women's Romances. What Laurence offers is indeed partial: we read her for the insights she has into the people she knows.

Am I being ungenerous? No. For all her flaws, Laurence — like the other Lawrence (D.H.) — knows the heart. She is not afraid to be old-fashioned or gutsy. She is not afraid to sound sentimental or confused. Her books have feeling, hard-won and real. And though that may not be much, her work is amongst the truest we have.

(1982)

"How to Act":
An Essay on Margaret Atwood

When art, religion, and finally even sex lose their power to provide an
imaginative release from everyday reality, the banality of pseudo-self-awareness
becomes so overwhelming that men finally lose the capacity to envision any
release at all except in total nothingness, blankness.

Christopher Lasch
The Culture of Narcissism

In all her novels, poems, and essays, Margaret Atwood has shown
herself to be an intelligent and technically accomplished writer.
Impassioned, wild, unexpected, epic, and merry are not adjectives
you could apply to her work, but controlled, careful, elegant,
witty, and (yes) sometimes beautiful, are. She is important, but not
for the reasons given by fawning journalists who have elevated her
to classic and cult status with an alacrity that is usually
reserved for politicians and sports stars. Atwood's popularity as a
novelist-poet-critic is a useful indicator of the values of current
fiction, criticism, and bestsellerdom.

Atwood is *fashionable*; but not fashionable in a superficial way.
She is the perfect recorder and personification of contemporary
literary and intellectual fads. She is a fashionable novelist *because*
her great subject is becoming. Where a novelist like Margaret
Laurence remains an upholder of classical values — a kind of
stoicism that, resembling Ecclesiastes, acknowledges change and
despair and contradiction, and yet insists on a resolute "I" —
Atwood writes from the heart of darkness, inside the flux. She is the
author of sophisticated self-help books, a writer working in what
could be called the Nausea-Romance school. Laurence mirrors
the present; Atwood is the present.

The Edible Woman, Surfacing, Lady Oracle, Life Before Man, and
Bodily Harm, begin in situations which are demented, diseased.
Atwood's characters are always damaged in some way. They are
either in flight from a kind of death-in-life or are fleeing toward an

imagined release. This is evident in each novel without exception, even when the tone of a particular work is parodic, as in *Lady Oracle*. The novels open with a vision of paralysis and despair, and go on to impute the cause of the condition to society and its mores (*The Edible Woman* and *Bodily Harm*), inner psychological states (*Surfacing* and *Life Before Man*), or to a combination of both (*Lady Oracle*). Atwood presents these states through the interiorized points-of-view of characters who are themselves the victims of the sickness. In this form of the *mal de siècle*, society is soulless and destructive, a character's craziness can be a sort of sanity, adjustment is derangement, breakdown leads to breakthrough.

Two quotations will clarify my point:

Terror of being blinded, frizzled up, destroyed. Clutch at myself. Fall. Fall away from Light to Darkness, from the Kingdom into exile, from Eternity to time, from Heaven to earth. Away, away, away, and out, down, and out.... Blood. Agony. Exhaustion of spirit. Struggle between death and rebirth, enervation and regeneration....[1]

Beginning to *think* again — to grasp, to connect, to put together, to remember....
Each forgetting a dismembering....
I must never forget again.[2]

No, these passages are not from an Atwood story. They are from R.D. Laing's "Bird of Paradise." I cite them only to show the roots of Atwood's thoughts and to demonstrate that her position has intelligible antecedents. Laing's proposition that schizophrenia is a metaphorical rejection of an unhealthy society is by now well-known. It is also a notion which found special vogue in the late 1960s and early 1970s, particularly in North America. What Laing was describing was a condition analogous to the Pauline idea of sin, of lifelessness, leading to insomnia and nihilism, the resentful destructiveness of the automaton. This is an important subject — some might say it is *the* modern subject — and that Laing's name came to mind for a strain of thinking that was acceptable in certain circles should not lead us to discount it.

Now we come to what Atwood does with the "disease" theme (which never quite qualifies as nihilism; but more on that later). It is well described in the early portions of her first two novels, carried on through the better collections of her poems, and expanded in *Life Before Man* and *Bodily Harm*. As you can see, there is a pattern here. And, interestingly, the elevation of Atwood to nationalist spokesperson and Serious Lit. denizen has kept pace with these publications. However, to give credit where credit is due, before proceeding I should point out that Atwood has shown in these books to be a minor master of the extended metaphor. The eating and starving motifs in *The Edible Woman*, the drowning and living water symbolism in *Surfacing*, the mirrors and mazes in *Lady Oracle*, the museum in *Life Before Man*, the cancer in *Bodily Harm*, display her good training as a lyrical poet. She is also capable of making these metaphors elegantly witty, particularly in the "fat" sections of *Lady Oracle*. These unifying images have a curious distancing effect, though. They have an artificial quality which tends to make her novels less passionate than ingenious.

As for "the disease," it is, in Atwood's 1960s terms, "power politics" that is the issue. "The disease" always begins in a type of passivity. The victim thesis is in fact Atwood's ruling *theory*. The unnamed narrator in *Surfacing* says at the end of her interior journey: "This above all, to refuse to be a victim" (p. 191). Earlier she says, flatly: "How to act" (p. 159). Yet that is not put as a question. It is stated ambiguously. She does not wonder about "How to live": she wonders about *how to act*. That is what is at the centre of Atwood's work. It is her overwhelming question. Every major character in every novel learns to go down, to make journeys into the interior, the mind, the soul, in order to rediscover and re-call consciousness and life.

The usual discovery in these works is that there is a zero at the heart of darkness. In *The Edible Woman*, Duncan and Marion share a final vision of snow and emptiness; *Surfacing* ends with nature "asking and giving nothing" (p. 192); *Lady Oracle* ends with a mirror of narcissism and a blankness; *Life Before Man* reveals nothing but the continuation of boring surfaces; *Bodily Harm* has the emptiness of political violence and inner hollowness. Yet the void allows rebirth. The cleansing, or catharsis (or the potential of these) is the result of an individual apocalypse. But the "final" transformation is never complete. Atwood's characters are left suspended over the void they have recently discovered, dimly conscious of new routes. How to act. This is at once a question, an exasperated shout, and a recognition that there is a way to live. Thus Atwood's women are ready to begin *ab ovo*, clean, fresh, and willing to become....

Once again, this is not a trivial issue. That it is probably Atwood's one and only theme should not be held against her. It is, after all, a theme that certainly reflects the present moment.

145

Yet: *how to act!* That is the issue of becoming, the self-help mentality which Canadians so dearly love, the program of imminent recovery and performance.

Atwood's initial presentations of death-in-life are usually penetrating and suggestive. Her writing glitters with a fine polish. It is marked by hallucinative twists and echoes from her inflexionless and tightly wrought verse. Sometimes the satire strains, the parodies become Ph.D. thesis material, and the style ends up precious and dry. For the most, it works. The *problem* with Atwood's characters and ideas and situations is that they are representations of pre-digested concepts of pure becoming. That is, her characters never achieve being. They are left with nothing on the edge of becoming something. Without exception her characters are always getting ready to live. They encounter the void and then find a way out, which turns out to be some gesture of ambiguous action. Stability and change in an interacting dynamic are necessities of existence. However, when one of these (change, becoming) excludes the other (being, stability), propaganda, bitterness, blindness, and the possibility of a new kind of falseness and another form of annihilation are not far off.

The insidiousness of the concept of becoming is that there is no centre. There is no reason to assume that Atwood's characters will not merely continue to become. In their shattering moment of insight, they do not recognize what they are, they get ready for the next step, the ultimate discovery of action. Preparation; flight; escape; search; avoidance; insight under pressure; but what next?

Thus Atwood's understanding of human psychology, while so artful and analytic on the surface of her work, is not far removed from the legions of self-awareness and self-discovery books found on the shelves of any major book-selling chain, with such titles as *Set Your Goals But Then Exceed Them!*, *Your Masterpiece — Yourself*, *Creative Divorce*, and *How To Be More Aggressive*. Hence Atwood's enormous popularity. She could never be a subversive writer — a rebel writing a No, in Thunder — because ultimately she has "nothing" to oppose. So quite logically, as each book has been published, we have watched her transformation from a sort of frizzy-haired Emile Zola to cover-girl, an ethereal doll on the pages of *Chatelaine* and *City Woman*. And all this has been implicit in the content and movement of her writings. Her characters never achieve anything other than partial being, the *appearance* of identity. They remain in a remarkably comfortable state poised somewhere between acting and nothingness. They become actors. (It appears that Atwood may have read a great deal of Sartre; but that is difficult to know for certain.) This state is, as it turns out, very flattering to the *Zeitgeist*, to those readers reared on Laing, collective encounters, "raised consciousness," primal scream, Marcuse, feminist *angst*, and EST. Although it could be that Margaret Atwood's greatest problem is simply that she's not Jewish. Then all the *angst* would have been understandable. She could have then had a cause, a reason for suffering and acting.

Atwood is so impressive in her use of allegory and sense of narrative rhythm, her clear imagery and self-deprecating wit, that it may appear to be malicious carping to insist on the unpleasant truth of what she is saying. Atwood has also let it be known in interviews and articles that she dislikes criticism, calling it "mingy-mindedness"[3] — or "the Canadian syndrome," which is our penchant for "whipping" writers once they become known. Atwood offered her startling insight in, of all places, the *Chicago Tribune*, in a country that has produced Norman Mailer, Gore Vidal, John Simon, Leslie Fiedler, John Gardner, Dwight MacDonald, Susan Sontag, Wayne C. Booth, Norman Podhoretz, James Atlas, Kate Millet, and Yvor Winters, and a multitude of other famous and infamous gunslingers, gangsters, iconoclasts, scourges, reactionaries, cultural aristocrats, and big-game hunters. That sort of comment by someone of Atwood's stature merely underscores my argument: she is not an opponent of anything in particular. She does not vivisect, and will not tolerate it in return. In short, *the authority of fashion depends on the premise that you do not question your own tenets.*

We might observe that the popularity of Atwood's books in certain Canadian circles seems (and I am, admittedly, speaking tentatively) to be a result of the enthusiasm of those readers who were raised in the 1960s. It would not surprise me if the majority of Atwood's most ardent admirers are professionals in the twenty-eight to thirty-five age group, the majority of whom are working for newspapers, magazines, literary journals, universities, the electronic media, and publishing firms — perhaps in or near Toronto. They are a generation that knows a lot about derangement, disease, subjectivity, becoming, political change, Marcuse, Laing, and Norman O. Brown. The electric elements of these thinkers are still current, of course. However, a trivialization has occurred: catch-phrases, vague notions, and handy quotables have been assimilated to become the modern fashion of the search for self-understanding. Subjectivity is enthroned; dissolution is vicariously glamorized; endless becoming is legitimized; the Culture of Narcissism looms.

Now, here is where Atwood's writing of self-help books for the sophisticated comes in. She is a popularizer of "the disease" and its cures. She has, more than any other contemporary Canadian author, written about that *angst*, and she has, with some courage, tried to find an answer. As she writes at the end of *Survival*:

Have we survived?
If so, what happens *after* Survival? (p. 246)

Her answer? Re-creation: make yourself over. The Nausea-Romance.

Observe, for example, the cover of *Chatelaine* (January, 1981). Beside an air-brushed photograph of a smiling Atwood, you find these headlines: YES! NOW STERILIZATION IS REVERSIBLE; FASHION DOS AND DON'TS IF YOU'RE SHORT, MEDIUM, TALL; 4 TERRIFIC DECORATING SOLUTIONS TO CLOSET CLUTTER; 30 GREAT TASTING RECIPES; CHATELAINE'S HEALTH CENTRE, THIS MONTH — A BIOCHEMIST RATES 10 WINTER FITNESS HOW-TOS. In the opposite corner: WOMAN OF THE YEAR 1981, MARGARET ATWOOD, SUPERWRITER! The article opens with these sentences:

Margaret Atwood, that brilliant, beautiful, man-hating but well-adjusted, somehow plain though slightly exotic, happy and successful albeit weird and pessimistic but really perfectly *normal* cultural icon, is her own best character. But not one she will take credit for creating.

I cannot believe that Atwood welcomes that sort of thing; yet over a year later in the same magazine (May, 1982), we find "Chatelaine's Celebrity I.D." on Atwood, clearly written with her knowledge and participation. The article provides us with vital information about her height, weight, eyesight, hobbies, and favourite movies. It would seem that she prefers this kind of "critical" writing to "mingy-mindedness." That and of course the usual academic analysis churned out by brainwashed "Can.Lit." teachers and students. *How to act*. Indeed.

One remembers the jolt *Surfacing* and *Survival* were for readers and critics in the early 1970s and how they seemed to symbolize the nationalistic fears and hopes of a generation of intelligent middle-class Canadians. As George Woodcock writes in "Margaret Atwood: Poet as Novelist":

I found the continuity [of *Survival*], the sense of an

extraordinarily self-possessed mind at work on an integrated structure of literary architecture, not only interesting and indeed exciting insofar as it concerned Margaret Atwood herself, but equally interesting and exciting as an index to the development of our literary tradition; a generation or even a decade ago, it would have been impossible to think of the Canadian literary ambience fostering this kind of confident and sophisticated sensibility.[5]

Yet the promise has not been fulfilled in the way Woodcock and others had hoped. Considering Atwood's natural abilities, it is important to speculate on why her novels and poems have descended to repetition and disappointment.

The repetition comes from Atwood's formula, which she has pursued from her first books to the present. The formula consists of the following: once you are a victim of the "disease," the only way back to health is through revolution — a *personal* revolution, as anything more comprehensive would be un-Canadian, and certainly dangerous. By positing a process of losing self and regaining self, the essential personality becomes unstable, fragile, vague. No balance is attained in her books, no tension, no contradiction, no otherness, no love, no recognition of wisdom or will. (Has Atwood read Nietzsche? No, I don't think so.) Atwood sets up a bleak vision in her works, often with some power, and invariably gives up, out, or in. She abandons her portrayal of modern rot, and then — because the vision seems to be too much for her — she rushes to embrace a new kind of tyranny — constant becoming. How to live life before man; "How to be a Creative Non-Victim"; the Survival guidebook; "Songs of the Trans-formed"; "Surfacing to Avoid Bodily Harm." Atwood shows people losing the world and then tries to regain it for them by offering glib substitutes. But as Margaret Laurence has shown, with greater honesty, you cannot escape what you are that easily.

Like most people who have had their "consciousness raised," Atwood has, as *Bodily Harm* discloses, discovered political commitment, particularly of a vaguely leftist sort, generally on the safe turf of anti-colonialism, anti-dictatorship, anti-violence, and anti-censorship. I am not negating the validity of her causes. As I am merely trying to point out, this just again expresses the accepted clichés of the moment in certain intellectual-artistic circles, and avoids the risk of exploring and revaluating human nature and human values. She betrays her independence of mind for a contrived cozy, and flattering self-image.

Yet I can hear the countering chorus reply that Atwood is all human nature in her novels and poems. We should not be confused. Atwood does not have a view of human nature. There is nothing stable or defined enough in her books to qualify as "nature." This condition is attractive to (and a reflection of) an age that avoids facing what we are, whose primary intellectual concern is to shower readers with pseudo-thoughts, with new theories and jargons that dress up old ideas and sell them as the latest goods. Atwood's avoidance of questions about human nature is very political, in more than one sense. As Camus explains in *The Rebel*, Marxist politics and historical determinism conceive of human nature as something infinitely changeable. It is a view of human society that always looks forward to the next step, the future tense, the new Jerusalem built out of the bricks of a decadent society. (Ernst Fischer's fascinating polemic, *The Necessity of Art*, provides an illuminating example of this kind of argument in its later chapters.) Superficially, Atwood's program is perfectly suited to that, which undoubtedly explains in part why the characters in her novels have a tendency to sound alike. It is remarkable to see how they have a similarity of tone. Examine the first page of *The Edible Woman, Surfacing, Lady Oracle, Life Before Man, and Bodily Harm*, and you will observe how one narrative persona could be replaced by one of the others. For example:

I know I was all right on Friday when I got up; if anything I was feeling more stolid than usual. (*The Edible Woman*, p. 11)

I can't believe I'm on this road again, twisting along past the lake where the white birches are dying, the disease is spreading up from the south.... (*Surfacing*, p. 7)

I planned my death carefully; unlike my life, which meandered along from one thing to another, despite my feeble attempts to control it. (*Lady Oracle*, p. 3)

I don't know how I should live. I don't know how anyone should live. All I know is how I do live. (*Life Before Man*, p. 3)

This is how I got here, says Rennie.
It was the day after Jake left. I walked back to the house around five. (*Bodily Harm*, p. 11)

These are all the *same* voice. There is not much which distinguishes them. Of course, if you do not have an adequate vision of human nature, then it follows that you would not have a sense of characterization as something objective and distinct.

Significantly, the same observation applies to the absence of a sense of environment in her urban novels, *Lady Oracle*, *Life Before Man*, and the early portions of *Bodily Harm*. Place Atwood's description of the city beside those of Joyce, Dos Passos, Baudelaire, Dostoyevsky, or Lawrence Durrell, and you will instantly see what is missing. These are her urban books, and yet where is Toronto, with its clean, slick city-streets? Where is its constant construction, its artificiality, its new technology, its big money? Where is the sensitivity to electricity, neon, and steel? These novels are devoid of the sights, sounds, speed, and tastes of contemporary city-life. Her characters wander in and out of stores and restaurants, museums and office towers, and only incidentally are we offered glimpses of what is out there — that feel and smell and texture and vision of concrete and glass, grease and swarming crowds, corporate commerce, buying and selling. Like her characters, Atwood's cities are phantoms. It could be that she has been reading a lot of Alain Robbe-Grillet and Nathalie Sarraute and the other French New Novelists. Yet it does not take much to see that the central fact of advanced technological cityscapes — of which Toronto is surely one of the greatest examples — is their spectacular decadence. The city is playground and asylum, theatre and sewer. Anything is possible because nothing stays still. *Innovation is motion.* The urban texture is such a complex entwining of simultaneous events — all of them man-made — that you could conceivably merely organize and present research and that would suffice to evoke the multiplicity of experience. But Atwood is strangely unobservant about our new experience. The only thing alive to her characters is their own mind and feelings. They are somnambulists. What we get from them, endlessly in each novel, are the precious convolutions of thoughts and feelings and reaction: "How I feel about this," "What I'm thinking now," "My response to him," and "How these people are dangerous." We find priggish introspection, deflating parody, and the fear of human engagement. (However, that may one day make Atwood an indispensible guide to the culture of Narcissism.) Nearly every character in every Atwood novel hides a wild terror of otherness, of the presence of others — usually men — and what they might do. Everyone else is powerful; her protagonists are not. When they break down, their breakthrough is to *more* self-consciousness. Atwood ably evokes the effects of city-life — rootlessness;

disembodiment; stunted emotions; hedonism; surface living; infatuation with extremes — and generally ignores the causes. Then by leaping to declarations of imminent action ("This is what will happen"), Atwood hopes to show that The Problem can be overcome and that a new being is possible.

The confounding fact is that — Atwood is capable of art. Take *Bodily Harm*. For all its repetition of familiar Atwood ideas, it could have been her best book. The imagery of the pornographic film, the punishment cells on the Caribbean island, the sarcastic references to "sweet Canadians," the intimations of death-in-life, the trendy talk of the Queen Street Torontonians, are rendered with precision. There are moments when you think you are on the brink of seeing something, that the author is about to go all the way. It is doubly disappointing when Atwood finishes with her "How to act" finale, as she imagines a new being offering eloquent outcries of a transcendent faith while flying off to greet the brilliant new dawn. You can almost hear the music. The *real* ending occurs three pages earlier, in the last scene in the cell with Rennie and Lora. So at the conclusion of a disturbing novel, Atwood falls back on her becoming habits, and "the interplay between ambitious perception and society,"[6] as Norman Mailer calls it, is replaced by a simplistic rush of rhetorical mush.

We have a last question to address: what happened? Perhaps something like this: personal anxiety, the consciousness of her position in vogue, and our own cultural-"critical" climate. Atwood consistently moves toward an attempt to see the world as it is, and then succumbs to the banal self-help determinism and the Canadian reflexive smirk. It is as if she stops because it would be imprudent to push any further. The often-heard accusation that Atwood is morbid and bleak is misdirected. Her problem is that she is not hard and critical enough. (I sometimes think that Atwood aspires to be an Anglophone Marie-Claire Blais, or better yet, the Canadian Joyce Carol Oates — two contemporaries who do go all the way, and have managed to resist faddishness.) It is amazing to watch how time and again Atwood will go for the flip remark, the tight-lipped murmured suggestion, the parody that passes for satire, the political-sentimental "yes," the lyrical phrase that opts for polish and gloss. Rather than risk exposure, censure, or shock, she retires into a mist of acceptability and elegant form. As I've said, she apparently longs to be the opponent of society, but she cannot find anything too terrible to oppose. Yet the targets lie all around her, in every book, on every page, in every sentence. Let's not skim over what is at stake: to vivisect moral issues is to take a considerable chance. Atwood's failure may once again be our own — that habitual Canadian dedication to "niceness," the second-best, and the ironic self-put-down. It may also be uniquely contemporary — the dilemma of honest action in a surrounding maze of reflecting mirrors. Anger is no guarantee of art either. However, though Atwood's accomplishments are many, a sign of a writer's impact and worth are the furies he provokes, for — as it has been said — a serious writer in a bad age who does not make powerful enemies is either flattering the *Zeitgeist* or risking early obsolescence.

Still, *Surfacing*, parts of *Lady Oracle*, and a number of poems, "Mushrooms" especially, have their rewards. They hold out the hope that she may break through the shackles of her position in "Can.Lit." and those retouched shots on the covers of the chic magazines which are dedicated to the triviality she has herself parodied, and become the writer of contemporary suffering that she clearly has the talent to be. Who knows? Atwood may yet survive her own image.

(1982)

Addendum to Atwood

Has Atwood survived?

Since my writing of "How to Act," Atwood has published two more books, *Second Words* (1982), a volume of essays, and *Murder in the Dark* (1983), a collection of "short fictions or prose poems." Once again, the technical polish in both books is exquisite: the writing is slick, artful, intelligent. *Second Words* shows off her ability to write effortless articles: "Canadian Monsters" is one of her better essays, as is her sarcastic defense of *Survival* in "Mathews and Misrepresentation." *Murder in the Dark* indicates a step into post-modern hijinks, with the Barthes-Barth stamp. Note especially "Happy Endings" and "The Page." The usual Atwood first-person voice is present in "Autobiography." The self-help signature appears in "Mute": "Whether to speak or not: the question that comes up again when you think you've said too much, again" (p. 49). Rather than developing her moral imagination radically, she seems to be flying, with great haste, from the questions. Witness her uneasy public statements about not being a role model ("No, thank you very much," CBC Radio, "Stereo Morning," October 1982), and her tongue-in-cheek review of her own *Second Words* in the *Globe and Mail* (November

20, 1982), where she writes three inadvertently self-revealing remarks: "Margaret Atwood, one suspects, may be a front for a committee...." "It has long been our opinion that 'Margaret Atwood' ('Peggy' to her friends), purported author of some 20 books, does not really exist...." "[*Second Words*] is a perfectly safe Christmas gift...."

As all this fiddle suggests, Atwood is at a pivotal point in her career. Choices beckon. It will be interesting to see if she makes them.

(1983)

Odd Man Out

"*Father, remember, we're living in the twentieth century!*"
"*The twentieth century! I could pick a century blindfolded out of hat and get a better one!*"

Dialogue from
Billy Wilder's film Sabrina

Et ignotas animum dimittit in artes

Ovid, Metamorphoses, VIII,
188

I

Stately, the Master emerges from the side door of Massey College, laughing to himself, a large panama hat set jauntily over his longish grey-silver hair, a bulging bag of groceries under his arm. He walks up to his low sleek car parked in the driveway; stopping, he reaches into the pocket of his trench coat, feels around, and with a flourish, as if producing something of infinite value, pulls out a set of silver keys on a ring. Selecting one he places it in the trunk lock, turns it so that the trunk pops open. Inside there are grocery bags jammed with green vegetables and fruits, a cooler, canned foods, bottles, and cardboard boxes. He bends over to observe. His gaze is concentrated and still.

He seems smaller than his pictures, not so bearish or magisterial. The figure he presents is rather gnomish and gentlemanly, if not courtly; yet there is that uncanny look of a John Ruskin or a Thomas Carlyle, a late Victorian sage stepping inexplicably into the wrong place, the wrong era. The grey beard streaked with black wisps, the silver hair, the deliberately archaic appearance (if you were to use a more contemporary simile, like some deliberate combination of Colonel Saunders and Santa Claus) suggests Personality, Playfulness. And the eyes: they are preternaturally alive; laughing lines cut deeply around them, the bushy eyebrows arching upwards in a satanic twist. With that look you can never be certain if he will laugh with you, or at you.

The Master begins arranging things in the trunk. Everything is fit; everything has its place. It appears as if he is preparing for a visit to the country, a long weekend away from the obligations of a University. His hands move in conscious, deliberate arrangements, like a stage director's commands. He replaces one can of vegetables with another, stops to ponder; then pushes a small box from the left to the right.

Someone hails the Master from the iron gates, the entrance to the exclusive monastery-like college. He jerks up. His head seems at that moment much too large for the small body; and the beard and the wide hat enhance the sense of top heaviness. The hall porter silently waves a blank white piece of paper. The Master waves back; then gazes reflectively at the contents of the trunk. He reaches inside; he pauses; then he bends down again, as if into a bottomless box, seemingly reaching for something buried deep inside.

II

A descriptive paragraph, selected at random, to start:

> It is not hard to discover why the word "quaint" is so often applied to Salterton by the unthinking or the imperceptive; people or cities who follow their own bent without much regard for what the world thinks are frequently so described; there is an implied patronage about the word. But the people who call Salterton "quaint" are not the real Saltertonians, who know that there is nothing quaint — in the sense of the word which means wilfully eccentric — about the place. Salterton is itself. It seems quaint to those whose own personalities are not strongly marked and whose intellects are infrequently replenished.

To interrupt: I shall ask if you can identify the century in which this was written, in what country, and who the author is. Any answers? No? Let's continue:

> Though not a large place it is truly describable as a city. That word is now used of any large settlement, and Salterton is big enough to qualify; but a city used to be the seat of a bishop, and Salterton was a city in that sense long before it became one of the latter. It is, indeed, the seat of two bishoprics, one Anglican and one Roman Catholic. As one approaches it from the water the two cathedrals, which are in appearance so strongly characteristic of the faiths they embody, seem to admonish the city. The Catholic cathedral points a vehement and ornate Gothic finger toward Heaven; the Anglican

cathedral has a dome which, with offhand Anglican suavity, does the same thing. St. Michael's cries, "Look aloft and pray!": St. Nicholas' says, "If I may trouble you, it might be as well to lift your eyes in this direction." The manner is different; the import is the same.[1]

How does the manner strike you? Can you identify it? George Meredith? ... A companion of Arnold Bennett's perhaps?

It is our own Robertson Davies. The passages are from his first novel, *Tempest-Tost*, published in 1951 by Clarke-Irwin in Toronto. It is the first book in what has been dubbed "the Salterton Trilogy." The three volumes are in print and are available at most bookstores, for those of you who are curious as to what Canada was like in its proudly Tory and colonial period.

Davies has surely read George Orwell on style, so his prose is plain-spoken, economical, and elegant. Yet the decorum is so much in place that the paragraphs quoted above resemble excerpts lifted from a textbook on "How to Write Good Prose Fiction," circa 1914. There is no fractured or idiosyncratic syntax, no disintegrating or perverse points-of-view, no obfuscations, obscurities, obscenities or ambiguities. The tone is lofty and amused, the manner arch; indeed, as if the authorial mask itself has a raised eyebrow. You sense something of a *Magister Ludi* here, a didactic intelligence instructing us about the proprieties of life. As we know, Davies is a playwright and... but no. Let us move on, past the two other novels which comprise the "Salterton Trilogy," *A Mixture of Frailties* and *Leaven of Malice*, to something more substantial.

I am sorry to give short shrift to Davies' early novels and plays, but these works do not have much to offer other than indirect testimony to the struggle of a gifted writer in what must have been an unresponsive and provincial milieu. However, when the role model shifts from Stephen Leacock and Victorian comedy, we find something completely different:

Our village was so small that you came on it at once; it lacked the dignity of outskirts. I darted up our street, putting on speed, for I had looked ostentatiously at my new Christmas dollar watch... and saw that it was 5:57; just time to get indoors, wash my hands in the noisy, splashy way my parents seemed to like, and be in my place at six, my head bent for grace. Percy was by this time hopping mad, and I knew I had spoiled his supper and probably his whole evening. Then the unforeseen took over.[2]

Are we in another author's world? No, the writing is from Robertson Davies' novel *Fifth Business* (1970). But the certainty of the action, the diction, the witty tone, and the narrative rhythm indicates an imaginative and technical leap of considerable grace. The style is conventional and conservative. Again we are a long way from *Death on the Installment Plan, The Sound and the Fury* and *Women in Love*, or for that matter *Mr. Sammler's Planet* and *Deliverance* (both published in 1970). But we should not be insensitive to the subtle hold here: the technique has been properly subordinated to plot and character.

The narrative voice in that quotation belongs to Dunstan Ramsay, the guide to the first volume of a second series of novels called "The Deptford Trilogy." He is a teacher, a writer and biographer, an expert on saints, a distinctive Ontario-Upper Canada personality. Ramsay is an ironic, educated presence who speaks in what Ramsay himself refers to as "the Plain Style." This style is described in *The Manticore* (1972), volume two of the trilogy:

> Furthermore, he [Dunstan Ramsay] wrote well. I knew because he had been my history master at school; he insisted on essays in what he called the Plain Style; it was, he said, much harder to get away with nonsense in the Plain Style than in a looser manner. In my legal work I had found this to be true and useful.[3]

The description is supplied by David Staunton, the son of Percy Staunton in *Fifth Business*. (Staunton is undergoing a Jungian analysis at the time of this disclosure.) We can infer that the author would probably not be adverse to having his verbal manner characterized as being in "the Plain Style" although Davies' style is richer than "Plain" suggests. Taking our cue from these quotations: the Davies' manner is distinguished by elegance, a consistent tone, clarity, and rhythmic balance. But lest we forget: "Yes — oh dear yes — the novel tells a story," E.M. Forster acknowledges in *Aspects of the Novel* (1927). As Davies declares elsewhere: "I think of an author as somebody who goes into the marketplace and puts down his rug and says, 'I will tell you a story,' and then he passes the hat. And when he's taken up his collection, he tells his story, and just before the dénouement he passes the hat again."[5]

I do not emphasize Davies' style lightly. When he locks into the right words and rhythms, the stories gain clarity and power. "The Deptford Trilogy" is about the pursuit of *claritas* ("claritas": brilliancy, bright), the world of wonders illuminated with a visionary lucidity. Davies is a mental traveller. His fictional worlds are "large spiritual adventures,"[6] and his characters are always involved in a quest of some sort. Every quest begins with a question, and Davies' leads his characters toward climaxes which deal with the mystery of illusion and appearance. His major novels are journals of spiritual journeys, which, interestingly, begin with actual questions. The first pages of *Fifth Business*, *The Manticore* (1972), *The World of Wonders* (1977), and *The Rebel Angels* (1981) contain rituals of call and response. Davies' blatantly Tory and didactic work is a play entitled, appropriately, *Question-Time* (1975), which is prefaced by an interview where the author answers such overwhelming queries as "*What do you think your play is about?*" He replies: "It is about the relationship of the Canadian people to their soil, and about the relationship of man to his soul. We neglect both at our peril."[7] Davies' pursuit of "claritas" has thus led him toward an eccentric brand of questing. *Fifth Business* and *The Manticore* especially, are cunning polemical essays on the question of personality, behaviour, and beliefs.

Nevertheless, for a series of trials, Davies' novels are astonishingly static. The stories themselves have action, frequently violent, rarely (very rarely) sexual. Indeed, they are mostly narrated from a sitting position. *Fifth Business* purports to be a letter from a school-master to his head-master, cast as an "apologia pro vita sua"; *The Manticore* is almost entirely a dialogue between a patient and his doctor (both seated); *The World of Wonders* is a series of rotating monologues uttered by several narrators who are (usually) sitting down at the time. *The Diary of Samuel Marchbanks* (1947) and *The Table-Talk of Samuel Marchbanks* (1949) are musings (fitfully amusing) kept by what seems to be a seated ruminator. *The Rebel Angels* is constructed out of diaries, letters, manuscripts and recorded dialogues, composed by characters who are not engaged in any physical activity, like walking, exploring, fleeing, killing, riding on a train or making love at the instant of composition. The stories do not happen in process. They occur at a distance. Thus the narrative technique in Davies' mature undertakings revolve around speakers who are themselves mental-questors. How a speaker is positioned indicates authorial bias, and perhaps a cultural-social bias, too. Hemingway's speakers are usually doing something: like their author, and like America, they crave action. Davies' characters recall and analyze action, generally from a table or study desk. They reflect on what has happened in the same intelligent, slightly eccentric way that their intelligent, slightly eccentric author-professor would. Therefore: *Davies may be the personification of the classic Canadian novelist* (Upper Canada-WASP division).[8]

Which is a roundabout way of saying that Davies' novels and plays are moral lectures. He is an editorial artist. His work is invariably cast as rational, deliberate monologues or extended, almost Socratic, dialogues, or a mixture of the two. They are not related in the ranting, rambunctious way of Faulkner's *Absalom, Absalom*, or in the parodic manner of the "Cyclops" and "Ithaca" chapters in Joyce's *Ulysses*. Davies' talk is cool and sophisticated; he is the learned teacher as novelist and playwright. Also, the lectures come from a writer whose mind is mostly *made up*. He knows where he is leading you. "I am a plan-maker," he has said.[9] Narrative tension comes from the well-made mystery plot. *Fifth Business* culminates in a murder (which may be a suicide); *The Manticore* and *Question-Time* with a journey to the interior-underworld; *World of Wonders* with revelations of identity. Davies' stories are literally contrived. He is a great lover of artifice. "A wright is an artificer," Davies comments, "a handicraftsman, and anybody who sets to work to write a play should try to be a craftsman or he will almost certainly come to grief."[10] Note how Davies puts that remark: it is a stern editorialism uttered by one who wears the mask of a cultured detachment.

An artist whose mind is (mostly) made up will inevitably lean toward games-playing. A man with a plan builds labyrinths to contain the monsters of his imagination. Davies writes under the sign of Daedalus. And Dedalus (Stephen): there is more than a touch of James Joyce in his concoctions. Davies has been lionized by critics who enjoy an intelligent puzzle when they see one. He belongs in the company of the fictional teasers and formalists, like Nabokov. There are even vague shades of Borges in his antics: in 1970 Davies distributed seventy-five copies of "The McFiggin Fragment," purportedly a portion of Stephen Leacock's diary, to a gathering of scholars at a Leacock Symposium; until Davies confessed that the manuscript was a hoax, the learned crowd believed in its authenticity.

Yet the influence of Carl Jung on Davies has been stressed so often by sober and diligent exegetes[11] that you might think Davies' writings form an apology for the ex-Freudian from Zurich. (See *The Smaller Infinity: The Jungian Self in the Novels of Robertson Davies* by the aptly named Patricia Monk.) They do not. Anyone can see that the symbols Davies takes over are obvious and functional. "Jung gave me courage," Davies writes in his essay, "Jung and the Theatre."[12] A rudimentary knowledge of Jungian thought will suffice to understand what Davies is doing. The author invariably explains his meanings through the essays of his characters: Dunstan Ramsay and Liesl are well up on mythology, theology and psychoanalytic theory. Davies gratifyingly supplies the required modernist paraphernalia: labyrinths, demons, religious rituals, saints, caves, magicians; and these symbols and figures form a double-plot of echo and allusion. This gives his work a sense of recurrence. The dead are not dead in Davies' land. He is a past-master, returning us to the roots, the centre of the labyrinth, and his novels "dream back" to restore a balance to the world of wonders. (Interesting item: James Joyce took his mad daughter Lucia to see Jung in Zurich and was displeased with the "Reverend Doctor Jung," leaving soon after with the intention of psychoanalyzing his daughter on his own.[13])

What saves most of Davies' examinations from precious nostalgia and the self-regarding fictions of the "fabulists" are the four cornerstones of his artifice: his conservatism, his faith in the educational power of "the Plain Style," his sense of a public, his fondness for telling a story. Further, the quotidian exists for Davies. His descriptions of World War I in *Fifth Business* (compare them to Timothy Findley's *The Wars*), the London theatrical scene in *World of Wonders*, and the magic acts throughout "The Deptford Trilogy" are vividly handled. He remains *unfashionably* attentive to the world, indicating moral choices, giving us a feel for the fullness of experience.

III

Artifice, hoaxes, theology, Jung, well-tempered speech, balance, clarity, a mind made up.... Where does it all lead? Well you might ask.

It leads to "morality and hilarity." Which is likely to be a surprise for the humourless "Can.Cultists." "It is so easy to be solemn," G.K. Chesterton once said, "it is so hard to be frivolous." Davies is a comic writer; and I do not mean he is a humourist. He cons the audience with his dandy-Royalist mask, then his comic sensibility balances the world's tensions with deflecting irony and tolerance, and a recollection of our historical-mythical roots. *"The very essence of comic art — the stasis of comic 'joy' as Joyce himself might have said — is found in the living balance, the poise between vital uncertainties and unanswered questions which constitute, for a classical temper, the authentic mystery of life."* Thomas Merton[14]

Of all Davies' non-fiction work, it is *A Voice from the Attic* (1960) that outlines this view. Again the authorial tone in *A Voice* is elegant and intelligent. The Davies' strategy of opening with a question launches the Prologue: "A voice, certainly — any book is a voice — but why from the Attic?" (p. 3) He answers slowly, as befits a teacher:

> Statesmen are fond of stressing Canada's role as a mediator between the United States and Great Britain. Sometimes for us in Canada it seems as though the United States and the United Kingdom were cup and saucer, and Canada the spoon.... I am a Canadian, and of Canada one of our poets, Patrick Anderson, has said:
>
> ...I am one and none, pin and pine, snow and slow, America's attic....
>
> — and that is why this is A Voice from the Attic.

"A Voice from the Attic" is Davies' own *ex*-centric point-of-view: the voice of one somewhat off centre from the volatile neighbours, like "Fifth Business" and Canada itself, a character who is "odd man out," on the periphery of the true action.[15] If Robertson Davies were inclined to write manifestoes, becoming the Grand-Dada of Canadian Letters, as it were, this book would be it; but the author is a misplaced Victorian (Edwardian?) gentleman, preparing to chat, and blasts and blesses would be a serious breach of decorum.

A core of common sense underscores his discussion of readers and books. Granted, the haughty tone wears out its welcome after awhile: there is finally too much of that "equi-poise"-Tattler tone. But when we come upon "The Hue and Cry after a Good Laugh," we find:

> ...a sense of humour is not a thing which we can control completely; many people, in painful situations, have been overcome by a sense of the ridiculous.... Such a man is no mere joker....

And a further revelation:

> It is this uncontrollable quality which shocks people who
> have very little sense of humour of their own, and as a usual
> thing they reserve their highest admiration for people who
> are demonstrably and reliably serious — which frequently
> means merely solemn. Perhaps this is because humour is a
> thing of intellect rather than emotion, and people in general
> are more impressed by emotion than by intellect.... *Humour is
> a civilizing element in the jungle of the mind,* and civilizing
> elements never enjoy a complete or prolonged popularity. (p.
> 217, emphasis mine)

This talk of civilizing elements will not strike a chord amongst
the apologists for delirium, dementia, and honest ineptitude, but
in our rational moments we have to agree. The passage exposes the
essence of Davies' tactics, especially when he goes on to discuss
"the uncontrollable quality of humour which makes it so
dangerous as a profession." A brief sensitive reading of Evelyn
Waugh and Aldous Huxley follows; then a passage on the
underrated novelist, Joyce Cary:

> Telling a story in the first person is not a formula for success in
> writing comic novels, but it serves the true comic novelist
> well, despite the often discussed handicaps inherent in the
> method. (p. 246)

Ten years before the publication of *Fifth Business*, Davies wrote
that Cary's *The Horse's Mouth* "is a triumph of impersonation" and
"part of an even greater triumph... a trilogy..." (p. 247). Prophetic
words; and perhaps a declaration of his plan. Davies explains
Cary's novels in terms of narrative shifts in point-of-view, each
book telling "part of the story as it appeared to the narrator, with
difference of emphasis... which make them seem to be three stories,
though in fact they are one. The trilogy is a triumphant exposition
of the truth that we are all, unwittingly, playing supporting roles
in each other's personal drama." That is "the Deptford Trilogy"
in a nutshell. On:

> The tragic sense of life, the human predicament, the "sense of
> otherness" — all the sable generalities which are brought out
> to justify works which are aiming at tragedy and which so
> often succeed only in arriving at gloom — are all apparent in

Cary's trilogy, but in its totality it is seen through a temperament which is serene, distinguished, and courageous, and so it emerges as great comedy.

"A temperament which is serene, distinguished, and courageous..." You could say this of Davies himself. He would clearly like it if we did. And why not? If we view Robertson Davies as a writer of "great comedy," then his novels, essays, plays, and his public persona can be perceived as having a well-planned shape and intent. He is pursuing "a lightening of the spirit, a reaffirmation of the splendour and sacredness of life" (p. 249). Surely not an unworthy objective for a novelist, even if our minds crave the dark urgencies of our own time and our preference is for more incendiary weapons.

So it should be as a comic-moralist that Davies stands or falls. And if you still doubt that his debt is more to Dickens than Céline, then here is a list of some of the names Davies has created for his characters: Eva Wildfang, Griselda Webster, Mrs. Caesar Augustus Conquergood, Solly Bridgetower, Prebendary Bedlam, Millicent Maude McGuckin, Samuel Marchbanks, Lieutenant Swackhammer, Miss Puss Pottinger, Amasa Dempster, Padre Ignacio Blazon, Hippolyte Delehaye, Liselotte Vitzliputzli (known as Liesl), Leola Cruikshank (also Crookshanks), Bishop Woodiwiss, Miss Tattersall, Toad Wilson, Tiger McGregor, Theophilus Mynors, Maitland Quelch (known as Matey), Pargetter, Maria Dymock, Roland Ingestree, Sir John Tresize, Joe Dark the Knife Thrower, Heinie Bayer and "his educated monkey" Rango, Zitta the Jungle Queen, Happy Hannah the Fat Lady, Smet Smet the Hippopotamus Goddess, Molza the Human Salamander, Urban Frawley, Mrs. Constantinescu, and Cuthbert Pengelly Spickernell.

The latest installment in the mental adventures of the "Maple-leaf Rabelais"[16] is *The Rebel Angels*. It is not a novel that announces itself with any charm. Here is a style that bores along with lofty contempt for the churning events outside its narrow walk:

Autumn, to me the most congenial of seasons: the university, to me the most congenial of lives. In all my years as a student and later as a university teacher I have observed that university terms tend to begin on a fine day. As I walked down the avenue of maples that leads toward the University Bookstore I was as happy as I suppose it is my nature to be.... (p. 12)

In the beginning I admit I felt there were things more pressing than *that*. Reading on, however, with a perfect contempt for the subject and the manner, we start discovering, after all, a place for the genuine. The dialogue between Paralabane, the intrusive demon who propels the narrative, and Maria Theotoky, the gypsy love interest, snaps into life:

> "I've ordered well, don't you think? [Paralabane speaks] A good meal should be a performance; the Edwardians understood that. Their meals were a splendid form of theatre, like a play by Pinero, with skilful preparation, expectation, dénouement, and satisfactory ending. The well-made play: the well-made meal. Drama one can eat. Then of course Shaw and Galsworthy came along and the theatre and the meals became high-minded: the plays were robbed of their delicious adulteries...."
>
> "Is this an introduction to the story of your life?"
>
> "Just about anything leads to the story of my life. Well, here goes...." (p. 61)

Marianne Moore once wrote that "we/ do not admire what/ we cannot understand" and Davies sometimes seems to be blithely sailing off to a Byzantium of his own idiosyncratic imagining. Yet by page seventy-one, following the first extended rant by Paralabane (*lecture* does not describe his harangues), we feel with that tingle reserved for contact with a real writer that this book is, my God, good. The novel has the polish and wit of an aesthetic and moral point-of-view. So after we are introduced to bawdy gypsies, dialogues about God, Paracelsus, and "the Druids" of the University, a sinister plot involving the theft of an unpublished manuscript by Rabelais, a possible devil (Paralabane) and his subversions amongst the new monks of the late twentieth century (the professors), and after we are treated to several narrators and conversations about the nature of good, evil, music, mysticism, ministers, murder, suicide, and mediaeval methods of removing fecal matter, we come to the fitting finale for a comedy: a marriage. *The Rebel Angels* resolves, perhaps too glibly, on the tension between good and destructive evil:

> "That is what lends splendour to a university," said the Warden. "Not these dreadful interruptions of the natural order."

"You lean always toward the light, Warden; perhaps both are necessary, for completeness."

"Quite so," said the Warden. "...it is good modern theology to acknowledge every man's right to go to hell in his own way." (p. 326)

The Rebel Angels has some of the calculated "well-made" plot twists of *Fifth Business*: there is a faint taste of recycling. The arch-English tones and formal dialogues seem wilfully out of touch with modernist writing. Nor are his satiric impulses toward society and manners especially savage or Swift. (Davies is, incidentally, only one year older than William Burroughs.) He must be the only living novelist whose characters always speak in colons and semicolons. But when we identify The College of St. John and the Holy Cross as the University of Toronto, and the microcosmic Ploughwright College as Massey College (4 Devonshire Place, Toronto, Ontario M5S 2E1) we know that the work is an *accurate* portrait of a conservative Canadian Institution. The inscription on the dining hall of the College reads:

Happiness is impossible, and even inconceivable, to a mind without scope and without pause, a mind driven by craving, pleasure or fear. To be happy, you must be reasonable, or you must be tamed. You must have taken the measure of your powers, tasted the fruits of your passion, and learned your place in the world and what things in it can really serve you. To be happy, you must be wise. — George Santayana

A thought for the day which could be this essay's epigraph. And the epigraph to Davies' oeuvre, as it recalls his concern for tradition, order, respect, and reason. *High Spirits* (1982), a follow-up of sorts, collects ghost-tales created for Massey College's "Gaudy Night." Hence Davies' latest work travels in the track set by many North American writers: the University as Universe (phrase courtesy of Gore Vidal) as in John Gardner's *Mickelsson's Ghosts*, Joyce Carol Oates' *Unholy Ones*, John Barth's *Letters* and *Sabbatical*, Rudy Wiebe's *My Beloved Enemy*, John Metcalf's *General Ludd*, and the best of them, Saul Bellow's *The Dean's December*. *The Rebel Angels* represents a logical step from "The Deptford Trilogy": it describes the walk away from current terrors and obsessions into a "second paradise," where contemplation of the positive light is only on occasion punctured by "dreadful interruptions."

Thus Davies' works are forged into an intelligible point of view. He is one of the few Canadian writers who can handle ideas and remain readable. There are times when Davies appears to be writing for an audience of former Northrop Frye students, but this can be attributed to a similar intellectual strain in these fellow University of Toronto authors. They show concerns with myth, Jungian archetypes, the collective unconscious, the transformation of the bare earth into a World of Wonders, recondite information, an underlying Christian orthodoxy, as well as contempt for things left, feminist, pop, vulgar, obscene, or "existential," not to mention electronic, apocalyptic, fragmentary, or desperate. But when we read Davies' best novels from the right wings, as it were, he can be regarded as a temporary antidote to contemporary *angst*. This "odd man out" is comfortable with his sly persona, and he has managed an oeuvre of slender means, but of unquestionable presence. At once comic and cold, his writings cannot make him a representative writer of the age. He is anachronistic, but with a deliberation that mirrors the times, rather than acts as a mindless reaction. The Davies' style is serene, almost unmistakable; who else would *want* to write that way?

But this is our "Question Time," and from some questions, we should request an answer. Pointedly, Davies' symbolic figure of the artist as con-man, Magnus Eisengrim (a.k.a. Paul Dempster, Faustus Legrand, and Mungo Fetch) answer all the questions I have been raising in his speech from *The Manticore* on fictions and what is (for him) the human comedy:

— Is one expected to take it seriously?
— I think it deserves to be taken more seriously than most biographies and autobiographies. You know what they are. The polished surface of a life. What the Zurich analysts call the Persona — the mask. Now, *Phantasmata* says what it is quite frankly in its title; it is an illusion, a vision. Which is what I am, and because I am such a thoroughly satisfactory illusion, and because I satisfy a hunger that almost everybody has for marvels, the book is a far truer account of me than ordinary biographies, which do not admit that their intent is to deceive and are woefully lacking in poetry. *The book is extremely well written, don't you think?*
— *Yes. I was surprised.* (p. 260, emphasis mine)

(1981-'83)

Mordecai Richler:
A Conversation on
the Philip Roth of the North

"How can you not be a satirist?"

**Juvenal, upon looking
at decadent Rome.**

Colleagues and critics have contributed to the following. Some of my debaters' remarks were taken from reviews in *The New York Review of Books*, *The Toronto Star*, *The Globe and Mail*, *The Toronto Telegram*, and the works of Wyndham Lewis, George Woodcock, John Metcalf, George Bowering, Robin Mathews and Charles Taylor. Footnote citations have not been given as this would rob the reader of immediacy.

Part One

With remarks upon satire, nationalism, reading and craft
Persons: Cuber and Will
Time and Place: Early evening. A bar.

Will: [sitting down and ordering a beer] I see you're reading a book, what is it?
Cuber: *Joshua Then and Now* by Mordecai Richler. It doesn't have a plot, its characters are stereotypes, and it reads like the other Richler novels I've read.
Will: That's a lot to say, considering you haven't finished it.
Cuber: *Joshua Then and Now* is *St. Urbain's Horseman* rewritten. Richler is a temperamentally ill-natured writer and this novel's yet another of his endless complaints. Worse, he thinks he's an American.
Will: Richler's a satirist, and satirists merely say in public what everyone else says in private. A satirist is *paid* to be obnoxious, while most people just do it for free.

Cuber: You're not excusing his bad-temper and bitter vision?

Will: It's his *role* to act as an accountant of hypocricies. Beside, I don't feel any nationalistic obligation to buy his books. He's readable. Which is a considerable accomplishment today.

Cuber: I'm not surprised you feel that way. Richler hates being a Canadian, and he regards everyone else as Victorians. It frustrates him to have been born into such a Waspish-colonial milieu. A feeling I know *you've* expressed on occasion.

Will: Richler doesn't hate being a Canadian. His books are *about* Canadians, so you can't accuse him of self-hatred. An iconoclast will often turn on the very thing he loves best, anyway. Yet I agree to some extent. While Richler's best novels, *The Apprenticeship of Duddy Kravitz* and *St. Urbain's Horseman*, are either set in Montreal or have their roots there, his conduct seems like the product of a rebel. With his independence and polemical scorn, he does seem... well, almost American.

Cuber: Are you saying it's a virtue to be a Canadian and yet have the attributes of an American?

Will: I'm saying he's been a success because his writing is alive. He's read in the United States, England, and Israel.

Cuber: Richler has sold out his Canadian cultural heritage. He is scornful of the advances that have been made in our literary scene. Worst of all, he vents his superiority in *The New York Review of Books*, *Atlantic* and *The Spectator*.

Will: What *is* the Canadian cultural heritage?

Cuber: It's *British* North America. The Tory tradition. The kind of nationalism outlined in Charles Taylor's book *Radical Tories: The Conservative Tradition in Canada*. It's a nationalism based on the particularity of regions, the genteel decency of a man loyal to his neighbourhood and to his British heritage. We're a conservative nation....

Will: But Richler is a Jew from Quebec who has lived in Paris and London! His first novel was published in England! He's a member of the Book-of-the-Month Club editorial division! He's worked on scripts for Hollywood movies! He has in fact written with great particularity about his "neighbourhood" — St. Urbain's Street. Richler has spurned the Canadian clubs in order to find a larger audience, and because he's primarily interested in humanity, history, and writing.

Cuber: What do you mean by writing? I don't understand.

Will: Richler isn't self-consciously literary like Saul Bellow. He's an informal entertainer, aware of his targets, like smug provinciality, whether Canadian or Jewish. He's an adversary, a completely professional writer and controversialist.

Cuber: I grant he's professional, but his personality keeps interfering!

Will: Personality's the essence of Richler's writing. He writes novels of character; they concern individuals and their society.

Cuber: Maybe, but I can't believe you consider Richler a stylist. Not in the class of Flaubert, Joyce, Beckett, or any of the high priests of "le mot juste."

Will: No, his novels aren't supreme examples of verbal and architectonic control. But they're thoroughly *written*.

Cuber: Do you believe we should consider style to be more important than national identity and feeling? What can you expect from a struggling culture?

Will: Well, some writers say you don't have to read or write to be an accomplished artist. All you need is raw desire, a warm heart and a good agent. And modesty. You can't forget that Canadian writers must be above all chaste, civil, and humble, just like everyone else. Or how everybody else *appears* to be. Most contemporary novels read as if anyone could write them, and almost anyone has.

Cuber: Are you saying that Canadian writing lacks sophistication?

Will: What passes for literary sophistication is often an indignant attitude, the support of a small clique, and a faddish philosophy picked up from Toronto via New York City — or pre-World War II Germany. Sophistication is a product of culture, of a vigorous intellectual milieu, of confidence and training. Richler's a strong aggressive satirist, as I said, and satirists are always aware of the magic of language, its killing and healing qualities. The satirist *violates* sacred sanctums with his words.

Cuber: But if Richler's the sophisticated satirist you say he is, why don't I find him funny?

Will: You can't predict the effects of humour. Some readers find Tom Robbins funny. I don't. I *do* think that *Cocksure* and *The Incomparable Atuk* are funny. There are set pieces in *Duddy Kravitz*, like the Bar Mitzvah movie, that are models of burlesque humour. But as I said, Richler is a satirist, which is a deadly serious business.

Cuber: Maybe I'm having trouble understanding what you mean by satire.

Will: There are tragic satirists, like Wyndham Lewis, and comic satirists like Mordecai Richler, and there's a great difference between the two. Robert C. Elliott's *The Power of Satire:*

Magic, Ritual, and Art explores the primitive antecedents of satire in ritual, incantation and cursing. Mr. Elliott also brings up the problems with the etymology of "satire." Some say it is derived from the Greek "satyr," which was a playful pastoral deity, half goat and half man. The Latin "satura" means "mixed bag," a hodge-podge. It seems to be the Latin word which underlines the English term. But as you see, "satyr" suggests a tone, "satura" refers to form.

Cuber: Richler couldn't be aware of this. He doesn't strike me as being extremely well-read.

Will: He has made reference in interviews to the influence of Evelyn Waugh and the eighteenth-century wits. However, Richler's vision is comic, not a dark one, and he seems to be moving toward some sort of positive humanist position.

Cuber: Richler doesn't have the range of Evelyn Waugh.

Will: All writers have limitations.

Cuber: Ah, you don't want to admit that his first books are dreadful! *The Acrobats* is like Malcolm Lowry and Céline ganging up on Hemingway, with a little *Nausea* thrown in.

Will: *The Acrobats* is a young man's book, the work of a self-conscious exile *about* exiles. If it didn't have Richler's name on it, *The Acrobats* couldn't be identified as his. His second novel, *Son of a Smaller Hero*, has good dialogue and the first tentative steps towards the finding of his main themes — the family, the salvaging of individual dignity, and love between a Jew and a Wasp.

Cuber: But you forget *A Choice of Enemies*, which is like a bad John Le Carré or Graham Greene novel. It shows his contempt for people too.

Will: Forget those works. Richler's first important novel is his fourth, *The Apprenticeship of Duddy Kravitz.* I've re-read the book several times and I'm amazed at how it continues to live. Richler's style is brash, rough, and his ear for the nuances of street-talk is superb. Characters are fleshed out through dialogue and action. The taut brevity is matched by a giddy humour.

Cuber: *The Apprenticeship of Duddy Kravitz* is mindless and derivative of American Jewish novelists, like Philip Roth. Duddy isn't redeemed by anything. He's a stereotype of the aggressive young Jew. And throughout the novel, Richler avoids moral judgement about his characters. We aren't given anything which is clear *or* profound.

Will: The moral judgements are in the reader's encounter with the characters and the images. All satirists are moralists. And Richler provides something incomplete, a mystery, which is art.

Also in *Duddy Kravitz* for the first time Richler finds his true voice and subject. He shows he's urban, or *urbain*. Satirists love cities. As André Breton said: "The Street... the only valid experience."

Cuber: Breton was the principal theorist of Surrealism. That's not relevant.

Will: But "surrealism" is in many ways a term for "the super-real." Reality brought up to sharp focus, to intense perception, which brings dislocation. What Breton was drawing on was the relationship between the city and the modern mind. The city is the human theatre *par excellence* because nothing in it is inhuman.

Cuber: There you're showing an urban chauvinism! As if the whole world were one big city!

Will: Well, Richler found his voice when he found his city — Montreal. Look at the titles of his books — *The Street, St. Urbain's Horseman*. For the first time, after Duddy Kravitz, Richler's writing achieves ambiguity, and on occasion a mad, super-real quality. Bellow has that quality in his break-through novel, *Henderson the Rain King*. So does Norman Mailer in his journalism.

Cuber: Those writers are Americans!

Will: But North American culture is *the* modernist culture and that speed, that sense of twisted perception, are part of the way writers record its reality. Accelerated ravages: we live time in a wink. Few Canadian writers seem willing to take that leap. But beginning with *Duddy Kravitz*, Richler begins to hear his time. Richler is not a surrealist, but the best scenes and images in that novel and his subsequent ones have a feeling of burlesque about them. The ambiguous portrait of Duddy shows us a character who alternately engages and estranges us.

Cuber: What you'd call ambiguity, I'd call cynicism. Also that "reactionary" quality you condescendingly refer to in Canadian writing is a reflection of the eminent sanity and detachment of our society. Ours is a country of polite, sensible and hard-working people.

Will: Well, to me, Canada is as bizarre a place as any. Wherever there's modernist culture, there are conflicts, uprisings, repressions. We're a computerized cosmopolitan nation.... And to live with the unfinished, the ambivalent, the contradictory, and to use these as a way of presenting characters and situations, is (by my way) the mark of the modernist mind. After *Duddy Kravitz*, Richler went on testing his new style in *The Incomparable Atuk* and *Cocksure*, and these novels move farther into the grotesque. However, Richler's second breakthrough occurs in *St. Urbain's Horseman*. It's still a satire on contemporary mores and history, but the farcical elements are subordinated to plot and character.

Cuber: You're avoiding the fact that Richler can't write a plotted book! They read as if they've been chopped up and stitched back together by a committee of editors. He has a mind full of clichés. [Takes out a notebook] I was frustrated by Richler's cosmopolitan arrogance, so I made notes. I've discovered his techniques can be reduced to a few tricks, a stock of characters and situations. Like:

1. A smart-ass narrator who is:

a) a hard drinker
b) a chain smoker
c) a world-weary cynic
d) trapped by a ridiculous circumstance
e) a frustrated Romantic or Idealist
f) vaguely Socialist

2. Memories of the Spanish Civil War.

3. Anecdotes about the difference between Jews and Wasps, usually with regard to sexuality.

4. A fat businessman, with a "stein" in his name and a cigar in his mouth.

5. Stupid Canadian Nationalists.

6. Duddy Kravitz.

7. Funny, fast-talking cops.

8. Obscene language and graphic sex to establish "flavour."

9. Unscrupulous businessmen and their flunkies.

10. Movies.

11. Funny, fast-talking Jewish parents.

12. Stupid Nazis.

Will: Most writers have stock footage of one kind or

another! You've a bad habit of looking for categories to dismiss an author! And there's one thing you don't mention. When Richler's inspired, his language *moves*. I remember a passage about the prostitutes at Cannes from Richler's *Notes on an Endangered Species*: "Modishly braless hookers, nipples by Eversharp, are rooted here and there, the empty coffee cups before them unfailingly lipstick-stained."

Cuber: That's not good prose. Not in the way that John Updike or Robertson Davies would write it.

Will: But you can feel the rhythm which keeps you moving from word to word. Also those "set pieces" you dismiss often succeed brilliantly. The movie scripts in *Duddy Kravitz* and *St. Urbain's Horseman* are hilarious. Duddy Kravitz himself is too good a character to dispense with after one novel. "The Catskills" in *Notes on an Endangered Species* is an exposé of a Jewish community, not a glib repetition. Finally, Jake in *St. Urbain's Horseman*, Joshua in *Joshua Then and Now*, and the Wasp wives in both books, are fully rounded characters.

Cuber: Saul Bellow uses stock footage and makes those repetitions seem like the unfolding logic of a mind investigating his world. *His* oeuvre has unity and depth.

Will: Bellow is a novelist of ideas. Richler is too street-wise to be that intellectual. Their only similarity is in their humour and their ability to use language as a weapon. In *Duddy Kravitz*, *St. Urbain's Horseman*, *Cocksure*, and *The Incomparable Atuk*, the prose rhythms seem to have been literally sharpened, so the books hurtle with a quick nervous power.

Cuber: Conrad said "Action is the enemy of thought." This slashing fast quality makes Richler's work thoughtless and glib.

Will: Don't go to Richler looking for Thomas Mann. He's a totem-smasher; in an icono*clast* of his own, as it were.

Cuber: You admit he's a negative writer!

Will: Richler knows that by opposition you prove the durability and vitality of the human spirit. The conclusions of *Duddy Kravitz*, *St. Urbain's Horseman*, and *Joshua Then and Now* are not conventional happy endings. They imply the possibility of friendship, family, and success, but at a *cost*. The readers must have some sophistication to understand Richler's polemical comedy is meant to heal and not annihilate. To be critical isn't the same as being mean and negative.

Cuber: I don't believe that being negative is good for readers or for other writers. That's perverse! Why alienate yourself deliberately?

Will: Skepticism can be a more effective device than a glib affirmation, given the needs of the society and the audience. Modernism itself is based on the constant battle of negation and affirmation. And don't forget, Richler's written best-sellers, which he wouldn't have accomplished if his books were not fresh and accessible. Anyway, why don't we compare him to some other well-known Canadian novelists?

Part Two

With remarks upon sentimentality, dullards, and the unreadable

Cuber: We're going to talk about Richler and his peers and predecessors in the Canadian novel.

Will: Some "Quick and Expensive Comments on the Talent in the Room."

Cuber: W.H. New commented that Richler didn't believe Canadian writing had a past or a future. He's been stigmatized as "the Bad Boy of Canadian letters." There's a lot of truth in this, especially when we compare him to those writers he attacked in "Maple Leaf Power Time."

Will: Comparison and juxtaposition are the modern critical methods. And since my concern is intelligence, language, perception, and the power of passion, we have to be aware of the company he keeps.

Cuber: You mean someone like Hugh MacLennan?

Will: A perfect specimen. Well, to be fair, Hugh MacLennan has shown himself to be, over the years, one of the few we could call a ground-breaker. He's shown in his novels, interviews, and essays that he's decent, didactic, and engagingly liberal. He's on every Canadian reading list, and has been instrumental in interesting the reading public in the indigenous subject matter.

Cuber: I'm sure you agree this is a good thing.

Will: Yes. Unfortunately, Hugh MacLennan is probably *the* novelist who best represents the Canadian self-image. He's a total bore. There's no point in denying this. MacLennan's novels drone on for uncalled-for lengths, sometimes working up to a virtual frenzy of solemn outrage. *Two Solitudes* is respected more for its statement about our society than for its art.

Cuber: A harsh appraisal. I heard a sound moral voice in *The Watch that Ends the Night*, *The Return of the Sphinx* and *Voices in Time*. And there are parts of his books which live. He is a prolific essayist and has a nice self-deprecating humour. Surely being a ground-breaker counts for something.

Will: I'm being ungenerous towards someone whose public image is honest and long-suffering. But reading his novels is an exercise in a reader's patience. I'm certain literary students wouldn't read him if they didn't have to.

Cuber: What about a novelist I admire, Morley Callaghan?

Will: Another good-intentioned, intelligent, tireless bore.

Cuber: That's really unfair. His early short stories are superb, and his work is known in the United States and Europe. He's the father of the modern realistic novel in Canada. *That Summer in Paris* is an entertaining memoir about a period in twentieth-century letters you feel nostalgic for. Do you remember Edmund Wilson's judgement in *O Canada* that Callaghan was Canada's greatest writer?

Will: But that judgement was made before Richler, Laurence, Atwood, and Davies were writing their mature works. You have to remember how Wilson played St. Paul to the savage messiahs of the so-called Lost Generation. Whatever Wilson said, Callaghan's a writer of predictable stories. I grant that when he was hobnobbing for... what was it? five months?... with the Last Romantics, he was writing well. And yes, I enjoyed *That Summer in Paris*, but because of the subject matter, not the meagre style. He's a novelist with a strangely placid sensibility.

Cuber: Let's shift our ground to a writer who's very different — Rudy Wiebe.

Will: The Albertan Solzhenitsyn. *The Temptations of Big Bear* is a favourite among nationalists. John Moss calls it the great Canadian novel.

Cuber: It *is* a fine, ambitious work.

Will: It's certainly ambitious. *The Temptations of Big Bear* has passages which are so vivid you get a glimpse of what the novel could have been if Wiebe had made his prose "merely" readable. Do you recall the Frog Lake Massacre scene? A superb set-piece. But so much of his writing is humourless and puritanical. *The Mad Trapper* indicated a surprising falling-off, although *My Beloved Enemy* may be an attempt at some rebirth into the twentieth century. Wiebe has tried to be a historian, mythographer, theologian, visionary and storyteller, and that's admirable. Yet reading him is an ordeal, with few rewards.

Cuber: Wiebe's a passionate moralist and a man of potential. He's not taken in by cultural jingoism. Further, he's the only

Canadian novelist with a sense of the epic. *My Beloved Enemy* is a *visionary* epic....

Will: But in his two best-known historical novels, *The Temptations* and *The Scorched-Wood People*, his writing is too often ponderous. He wandered into the thick under-brush of Faulkner and Melville and never really came out.... Can we move beyond the Valley of the Dulls?

Cuber: You're displaying that mean spirit you sometimes criticize in Canadian culture. And what you're offering are passing remarks. It isn't criticism. The writers you're dismissing deserve more.

Will: These writers have their biographers and bibliographers. They don't need my admiration. But there's so much that has to be done before we can begin to discuss the state of things perceptively. Without a house-cleaning, we'll never have a sense of perspective.

Cuber: What is it you need, then?

Will: I'm looking for a writer you can read, learn from, grow up inside, someone full of risk and daring. A rich humanity. A full career. If you can't read these people then what's the point? Dead writing tires my eyes, dulls my sense of things, and kills the spirit.

Cuber: You're not arguing art for art's sake?

Will: I'm arguing art for *our* sake. To write is to enter into the verbal energies of the past, present, and future. If you can't turn to the artists for verbal perception and exploration, where can you turn? Besides, I like energy. Lightning. Thunder. I like the iconoclasts. The ones who don't have their minds made up. Who amongst these writers has a sense of humour as explosive as Richler's?

Cuber: I agree with some of your sentiments, but I don't think they're appropriate to these writers. I resent your glib phrase about the Valley of the Dulls.

Will: There *is* a place for boredom in writing, you know. Baudelaire has written about "l'ennui," and Proust shows how boredom can be rendered aesthetically pleasurable.... But that's another matter.

Cuber: And I suppose you believe Richler is superior to our earnest authors who could benefit from real criticism, and not complaints. Besides, my criticism stands concerning the sentimentality and ill-nature in *Joshua Then and Now*. There's an acerbic adolescent in him, a snide side that's never matured.

Will: He's a sentimental writer on occasion, but he doesn't belong to the School of Sentimental-Naturalists in Canadian Letters.

Cuber: Who on earth are they?

Will: The Sentimental-Naturalists have one thing in common with the Group of Seven: they're better at describing nature than they are at describing people. Farley Mowat and a number of prominent poets would be appropriate members.

Cuber: I suppose you'd include Ernest Buckler? A gentle, introspective novelist.

Will: Yes, *The Mountain and the Valley* could be subtitled "John-Boy Walton Writes a Novel." Beautifully written, in a lush gushing way, although the novel has found its niche because the thematic critics can fit it into "Survival-Victim" and "Regionalization."

Cuber: I enjoyed *The Mountain and the Valley* because it gave me a sense of the isolation in this country. It's a sensitively written novel.... How about W.O. Mitchell?

Will: W.O. Mitchell is trying hard to be Mark Twain. He's charming, he's humble, he's old, he's rustic, he has white hair. The ultimate Canadian artist. No wonder Richler seems like "The Bad Boy of Canadian Letters" when you put him in that crowd. When I think about it, Richler suffers from not being located in his appropriate peer group — the Jewish-Intellectual tradition in North America. With Arthur Miller, Roth, Kazin, Layton, Irving Howe, Leonard Cohen, Harold Rosenberg, Delmore Schwartz.

Cuber: True. We may be discussing a class and cultural clash here. The genteel versus the Jewish. Yet let me answer what you said about Mitchell. He's written *Who has Seen the Wind?* And for those who know the west, it captures that feeling of growing up there.

Will: I'm sure it does. The only problem is that Mitchell has re-written his one good novel at least three times. I've read *The Kite, Jake and the Kid*, and *How I Spent my Summer Holidays*, and I think Baudelaire had something *else* in mind when he wrote "Genius is childhood recaptured at will...." Richler is funny, but he isn't a harmless charmer. He has no time for humility. He has hustling anger and wit, and a vision of moral ambiguity. Where's the critical spirit in Mitchell? Where's the sense of danger? the sense that we're part of the modern world?

Cuber: Mitchell's "spirit" is a modest one. You can't expect him to be Baudelaire! You're expecting the wrong things from these writers! You accused me of boxing people in, but that's exactly what you're doing! ...Alright, I'll change the subject. What about the Quebec writers, those who are writing in French?

Will: It's an area I wish I knew more about. We are definitely the Prisoners of Translation in this country. Language changes perception, as you know. Gabrielle Roy and Anne Hébert have written fine novels, as has Roch Carrier — *La Guerre, Yes Sir!* especially. The one I admire is Marie-Claire Blais.

Cuber: At last we agree about something. *Mad Shadows* and *A Season in the Life of Emmanuel* have poetic intensity.

Will: Her novels are *charged* in a fashion you don't often find. She is important because she is dealing with sexuality, suffering, and violence with courage and skill. She is one of the few Canadian writers with a sense of darkness. *Mad Shadows* was an astonishing accomplishment for a writer who was so young when she wrote it. The only work which disappointed me was *Deaf to the City*. I struggled for over six months to finish it. Perhaps my difficulty was because of Carol Dunlap's turgid translation, but I think my trouble stems from the fact that *Deaf to the City* is like an imitation of Márquez's *Autumn of the Patriarch* written by someone briefly afflicted with logorrhea.

Cuber: That's the danger of the avant-garde. To end up being obscure, in a void, speaking to no one. Like Joyce's *Finnegans Wake*.

Will: Subversion of common sense is indeed one of the strategies of the avant-garde. However, I doubt if that's what Blais was up to in *Deaf to the City*. Joyce is readable with patience and work. Do you remember how Joyce said that he expected you to spend the rest of your life reading one of his books? Anyway, technical experimentation doesn't have to lead you into the realms of the unreadable. *A Season in the Life of Emmanuel* has a style and form appropriate to its subject and remains rivetting as a piece of prose. Barry Callaghan's *Black Queen Stories* has a pyrotechnic grasp of language and form, and yet the stories still speak to us.

Cuber: There's nothing avant-garde about Richler.

Will: No, he never defies common sense, and his interests do not take him into arcane, revolutionary, or erudite areas.

Cuber: Do you think Richler compares with the other Canadian satirists?

Will: Who are they? Being a satirist in Canada must be a lonely job! There are... so *few* of them. I can think of John Metcalf as one writer with a gift. *General Ludd* has flashes of hilarious satire on the "Writer-in-Residence" syndrome. His impatient collection, *Kicking Against the Pricks* is on target some of the time. He's fond of giving indignant interviews — like this one. Other than Metcalf, I guess there's Leon Rooke's *Shakespeare's Dog*, and some newspaper columnists, and that's about it. But of course if you aren't an Optimistic-Romantic today, you're in trouble with your general readership....

Cuber: [after a long pause] Well, now that you've obliterated a major portion of the "Can.Lit." Pantheon, we should say something about Richler's limitations.

Will: After I have another drink.

Part Three

With remarks concerning the future of a novelist

Cuber: One of the difficulties I'm having with our discussion is that no conclusions can be made about a living author. Richler has published over twelve books, and none of them indicate whether he has the stuff to become an important writer.

Will: He already *has* some importance. Richler has a quick bright prose style. There are few contemporaries who can write dialogue as well as he can. Moreover, his novels have political and social dimensions. Richler is excellent on class relationships and the subtleties of social intercourse — on how people *sound* from certain areas of society, like St. Urbain Street and Westmount. He's written intelligently about political issues, like the PQ in Quebec and the question of separation.

Cuber: You've been implying you have reservations about him. I'm interested in hearing the negative side.

Will: There are hints in *Joshua Then and Now* of a blank wall he has run against. His essays particularly disturb me.

Cuber: You said you admire them!

Will: His essays are rarely concerned with literary and cultural matters in a deep way. Compare him to the two most accomplished essayists writing today, Gore Vidal and William H. Gass.

Cuber: Gore Vidal, the talk-show celebrity? William H. Gass, the academic? And again, they're Americans!

Will: His popular image aside, Vidal is a public writer, a wit and a satirist, sort of a combination of George Orwell and S.J. Perelman. He has a clear, precise writing style and an arrogant authoritative tone. His concerns are political, prescriptive, and rhetorical, and he has the formal training to back up his judgements. He digs into political backrooms, economics, psychology, history. He's a fearless critic of literary pretentions and inflated reputations. Vidal has changed over the years, too, becoming tougher, challenging his limitations and his readers.

Gass is Vidal's opposite. He's a contemplative essayist whose style is elaborate, erudite, imagistic. Gass can ease into the rhythms of a sentence or the sound of a word in an uncanny way. He has a mystical ear, as William Carlos Williams said of Ezra Pound. Both essayists are novelists who are concerned with Tradition and the contemporary scene. They are complete writers.

Cuber: Still! Vidal, with his cold nastiness and his politics, and Gass, whose ideas about language are almost scholastic.... How does Richler fit in here?

Will: Richler is primarily a journalist, so his essays are written for a specific audience. His article for *Atlantic*, "Oh! Canada! Lament for a Divided Country!" was a shrewd piece of cultural analysis, but it didn't penetrate into the roots of our problem. Increasingly, there's something stagnant about his prose. I read Richler's review of John Barth's *Sabbatical* in the *Saturday Review*, and was amazed at how lame it was. Was this the writer who said that George Woodcock was "sometimes useful, never necessary," and called *Maclean's* "an inspirational journal"? Has he forgotten the satirist's credo, that either everyone is satirized or else no one is?

Cuber: You've said that Richler is a modernist, and yet you've also said he's critical of society. *That's* a contradiction. You cannot be modern and critical of "the modern" at the same time.

Will: The great satirists are very divided men, which is the source of the tension in their work. Pound, Lewis, Eliot, Mann, Huxley, and Joyce sometimes considered themselves satirists — which suggests how flexible satire is. When a satirist makes war on the world, he examines the contradictions of his society and his time. However, a satirist is often a judge, jury and advocate acting on behalf of an intellectual community which may not exist. Some are forced into satirizing themselves, and we then are treated to the disturbing sight of that misanthropic rage turned inward. Richler sometimes lampoons his anger in the portraits he draws of his cynical heroes, like Joshua and Jake; however, *he*'s a writer who is more at odds with the external than the internal.

Cuber: I've no idea what you're talking about. What's this external/internal split?

Will: Richler is driven to see what the spirit of the age *is*. He doesn't try to escape its impact, nor does he offer lofty abstract sermons, nor does he romanticize the land or our former colonial status. If Richler is sometimes divided about his position as a Canadian writer, it's because he's chosen to be less naïve, less self-infatuated, and less daunted by reality than some of our authors.

Cuber: You talk about the "spirit of the age" as if it were something real!

Will: Have you never read Nietzsche, or his English-cum-Canadian-cum-European counterpart, Wyndham Lewis? *Time and Western Man* is an analysis of how the *Zeitgeist* — and that term came into common use through Spengler's *Decline of the West* — affects and reflects general states of mind. When you start reading cultural climates or trends through writers like Richler, you read the vehement signature of a time. Ours has been called the "post"-Einsteinian age.

Cuber: What typifies this "post"-age?

Will: Music. Speed. Blurring of self. Darkness. Separation. Solipsism. The sense that all's adrift from the past. That the future is hopeless. Ours is the age when everything has to be rethought. It's a time when intelligibility is imperative.

Cuber: I don't see Richler doing that.

Will: Well, he's getting there.... As we all are.

Cuber: You still haven't said what disturbs you about his writing. I wish you'd stop dodging my questions. I know you can't predict the upheavals in a writer's career. To be blunt, I don't see an infusion of new ideas into Richler's work.

Will: Yes, Richler's manner is so adroit he can cover up when he's not taking risks. He has his readers, he sells books, he's making money. Richler *has* a gift, but I suspect it's a small one. This was something I saw when reading *Joshua Then and Now*. It's a hard thought, though one writers must face at some point. However, Richler seems to have gone as far as his training and talent will take him.

Cuber: I'm surprised to hear you echo what I said earlier. You also seem to be suggesting that Canadian writers often *don't* go the distance. Novelists like Timothy Findley, Marian Engel, and Robert Kroetsch, have written good books. There are others who have potential, like Joy Kogawa. But you're raising an interesting point because the One Good Book Syndrome says something about the struggle of our national soul.

Will: It says something again about our terrible *timidity*. What would be the result of our search? Another self-help program, funded by the Canada Council and run by a committee? Perhaps we're not critical and exploratory for good reason. The fear of discovery stops us.

Cuber: You're repeating yourself.

Will: And I don't want to sound cynical either, because a reader who values energy can get something from Richler.

However, one-note instruments can perfect their range forever, and they'll sound great. After a while, you want the rich sound of a full orchestra.

Cuber: You can be a virtuoso on a one-note instrument. Look at Kafka.

Will: And if you're Kafka, no problem. But the first criterion for an important living writer should be that you can't foresee his or her next move. "Old men ought to be explorers," T.S. Eliot said. Richler isn't old, but I wonder about the solidification of his skill into the familiar.

Cuber: [reciting] "It is foolish to demand of an artist that he should command every kind of form."

Will: Who said that?

Cuber: Goethe.

Will: [laughing] Well, he was right of course.

Cuber: You've almost succeeded in convincing me that rebellion is important for the future of our culture. Maybe I should re-read Richler's novels... someday, anyway.

Will: Good, because we have *St. Urbain's Horseman*, *The Apprenticeship of Duddy Kravitz*, several fine essays, to a lesser degree *Cocksure* and *The Incomparable Atuk*, and the smooth entertainment of *Joshua Then and Now*. What more can I say? Richler makes us laugh, he is intelligent, he is a moralist, he is a *writer*. That could be all we need... for now. Anyway, it's time to stop for the night. We can continue our debate some other time. Agreed?

Cuber: Agreed.

(1983)

Notes

Part One

Marshall McLuhan, the Put-On

1 Marshall McLuhan, "Catholic Humanism and Modern Letters," in *Christian Humanism in Letters, The McAuley Lectures,* 1954 (West Hartford: St. Joseph College, 1954), pp. 49-67. See also "A Historical Approach to the Media," in *Teachers College Record*, Vol. 57, No. 2, November 1955, pp. 104-110.
2 Jacob Brackman, quoted in Norman Mailer's *Existential Errands* (New York: Little, Brown, 1972), p. 194.
3 For an example of these confusions, see *The Canadian Forum* issue, "Homage to the Runner: The Legacy of Marshall McLuhan," Vol. LXI, No. 709, May 1981, especially "McLuhan's Wordplay" by Wilfred Watson, pp. 10-12; Sidney Finkelstein's *Sense and Nonsense of McLuhan* (New York: International Publishers, 1968); and Jonathan Miller's *McLuhan* (London: Fontana, 1971). The last two books are negative evaluations of his work.
4 At the time of this writing, the only partially completed manuscript of *Laws of the Media* had not reached publication. Another essay could be written on the tribulations of McLuhan's long-delayed last book.

Fear of Fryeing: Northrop Frye and the Theory of Myth Criticism

1 Murray Krieger, "Northrop Frye and Contemporary Criticism — Ariel and the Spirit of Gravity," in *Northrop Frye in Modern Criticism*, ed. M. Krieger (New York: Columbia University Press, 1966), p. 1.
2 Quoted in Wayne Grady's "The Educated Imagination of Northrop Frye," *Saturday Night*, October, 1981, p. 21.

3   Northrop Frye, "The Instruments of Mental Torture," in *The Stubborn Structure: Essays on Criticism and Society* (London: Methuen, 1970), p. 17.
4   Northrop Frye, "The University and Personal Life," in *Spiritus Mundi, Essays on Literature, Myth, and Society* (Bloomington: Indiana University Press, 1976), p. 46.
5   *Ibid.*, p. 46.
6   Northrop Frye, *On Teaching Literature* (New York: Harcourt, Brace, Jovanovich, 1972), p. 4.
7   *Saturday Night*, October, 1982, p. 26.
8   Matthew Arnold, "The Function of Criticism at the Present Time," in *Selected Poetry and Prose* (New York: Holt, Rinehart, and Winston, 1967), p. 163.
9   *Ibid.*, p. 148.
10 Oscar Wilde, "The Decay of Lying," in *Complete Works of Oscar Wilde* (London: Collins, 1973), p. 970.
11 *Ibid.*
12 Oscar Wilde, "The Critic as Artist," *op. cit.*, p. 1039. Frye himself explores his debt to Wilde in the first parts of *Creation and Recreation* (Toronto: University of Toronto Press, 1980), pp. 5-25.
13 T.S. Eliot, "Tradition and Individual Talent," in *The Sacred Wood* (London: Methuen, 1960), p. 58. Frye's idiosyncratic reading of Eliot can be found in a largely overlooked book, *T.S. Eliot: an Introduction* (Chicago: University of Chicago Press, 1963), where he sketches in the intellectual context for Eliot's essays. Frye clearly identifies with the conservative, religious Eliot.
14 "The Decay of Lying," p. 977.

McLuhan and Frye: "Either/Or"

1   Letter to *Weekend Magazine* (*The Globe and Mail*), September 22, 1979, p. 9.
2   Northrop Frye, *Creation and Recreation* (Toronto: University of Toronto, 1980), p. 3.
3   Northrop Frye, *The Great Code* (Toronto: Academic Press, 1982), p. xi.
4   Søren Kierkegaard, *The Point of View for My Work as an Author: a*

Report to History, translated by W. Lawrie: newly edited with a Preface by B. Nelson (New York: Harper and Row, 1962), p. 35.

5 Marshall McLuhan, *Culture is our Business* (Toronto: McGraw-Hill, 1970), p. 64.

6 McLuhan and Frye were aware of their differences and often fired brief blasts at each other in their books. See especially *From Cliché to Archetype* by McLuhan and Wilfrid Watson (New York: Viking Press, 1970), pp. 15, 36, 85-87, 118. Frye's thoughts on McLuhan can be found in *Spiritus Mundi* (Bloomington: Indiana University Press, 1976), in "The Renaissance of Books," pp. 63-65; see also *Divisions on a Ground* (Toronto: Anansi, 1982), edited by James Polk, particularly in "Conclusion," p. 73, "Teaching the Humanities Today," p. 94, and "Definition of a University," p. 153.

Part Two

The Literary Ring

I. The Forces and Figures of "Can.Lit."

1 I have borrowed this phrase from Norman Mailer's *Advertisements for Myself*.

2 Read Jack Batten's "Truth and Consequences: The Art of the Libel Lawyer," *Quill and Quire*, August 1982, which inadvertently provides informative images of the machinations of these close-knit groups. The Victoria College Group is part of the University of Toronto, which is one of the major universities in "Can.Lit."

3 The "Top Ten Popular Novels" as (infamously) compiled by Malcolm Ross for the Conference of the Canadian Novel held at the University of Calgary, February, 1978, are:

1. *The Stone Angel*: Margaret Laurence
2. *Fifth Business*: Robertson Davies
3. *As For Me and My House*: Sinclair Ross
4. *The Mountain and the Valley*: Ernest Buckler
5. *The Tin Flute*: Gabrielle Roy

6. *The Apprenticeship of Duddy Kravitz*: Mordecai Richler
7. *The Double Hook*: Sheila Watson
8. *The Watch that Ends the Night*: Hugh MacLennan
9. *Who Has seen the Wind*: W.O. Mitchell
10. *The Diviners*: Margaret Laurence

Reported in the *Montreal Star*, February 20, 1978. Fortunately a list has not been made up for poets.

II. The University as Hidden Ground

1 My discussion can be read alongside Gore Vidal's in *Matters of Fact and Fiction* (1977), especially his essays "The Hacks of Academe" and "American Plastic: The Matter of Fiction." Vidal observes similar trends in the American literary scene. Personal correspondence with writers and editors in Europe indicates that the situation is apparent there, too. I should state that Irving Layton in *Engagements* provocatively explores the matter, as does Louis Dudek in "Academic Literature" in *Selected Essays and Criticism* (Ottawa: Tecumseh Press, 1978) pp. 1-3. Dudek reports on the condition in 1944.
2 Malcolm Cowley, "The New Age of Rhetoricians," in *The Literary Situation* (New York: Viking Press, 1954), pp. 3-22.
3 Quoted in "French Letters: Theories of the New Novel," by Gore Vidal, in *Matters of Fact and Fiction* (New York: Random House, 1977), p. 66.

A Climate Charged: The Intellectual Atmosphere in Canada

1 One of the leading diagnosticians of "the death of art" syndrome is George Steiner, who wrote in 1965 that:

"...there *is* a crisis of the novel. One knows the denials.... that neither writers nor readers of fiction are aware of any ominous condition. To which the answer is: yes, but.... the sense of disarray is perceptible. It is eloquent also in the lunatic economics of the fiction business." From "The Pythagorean Genre," in *Language and Silence*. (New York: Atheneum, 1967), p. 80.

I am delighted to report that Mr. Steiner did not take his own advice and has written an excellent novel, *The Portage to San Cristobal of A.H.* (1981).

2 Louis Dudek, Interview in *Quill and Quire*, September 1982.

3 The popular organs of criticism are individual studies and journals. Anthologies like *Contexts of Canadian Criticism* (1971), *The Canadian Imagination: Dimensions of a Literary Culture* (1977), and *The Canadian Novel in the Twentieth-Century* (1975) are practical collections for identifying drifts and themes. There are also handbooks, like the writer's section of the New Canadian Library (Michael Ondaatje on Leonard Cohen, Clara Thomas on Margaret Laurence, etcetera). The major magazines are *Canadian Literature*, *Essays on Canadian Writing*, *The Journal of Canadian Fiction*, and *Studies in Canadian Writing*, though most small magazines from *Rune* to *Writ*, carry reviews, articles and essays.

4 Wyndham Lewis, Introduction, *Men Without Art* (New York: Russell and Russell, 1964), p. 9.

5 Eli Mandel has continued this alarming habit in almost every essay he has written. I direct the reader to his informative essay "Northrop Frye and the Canadian Literary Tradition," in *Centre and Labyrinth: Essays in Honour of Northrop Frye*, edited by Eleanor Cook, Chaviva Hosek, Jay Macpherson, Patricia Parker, and Julian Patrick (Toronto: University of Toronto Press, 1983), pp. 284-297. In this piece Mandel clearly wishes to write something more critical about Frye's influence, and yet does not. A similar fate befell Louis Dudek. He began as an excellent critic, as his book *Selected Essays and Criticism* (Ottawa: Tecumseh Press, 1978) indicates; here the tone is tough; the knowledge wide; his approach personal and local and yet universal and public. As the essays progress through the years, the fury runs out; the insular atmosphere closes in; a strange bitterness takes over; and eventually he begins to sound like an apologist.

6 John Moss, "Bushed in the Sacred Wood," *The Human Elements*, Second Series, edited by David Helwig (Ottawa: Oberon Press, 1981), p. 161.

7 David Helwig, Introduction, *The Human Elements*, edited by David Helwig (Ottawa: Oberon Press, 1978), p. 9.

8 James Atlas, "In Praise of Dispraise," *Atlantic*, August 1981, p. 83.

Part Three

Raging Bull: The Poetry, Politics, and Polemics of Irving Layton

1 Irving Layton, "Niagara-on-the-Lake," from *For My Neighbours in Hell* (Oakville: Mosaic Press, 1980), p. 48.

2 From the author's "The Swimmer: An Interview with Irving Layton," *Conjunctions*, Spring 1984.

3 Quoted in "Heinrich Heine" by Michael Hamburger, in *Contraries: Studies in German Literature* (New York: E.P. Dutton, 1970), pp. 141-142.

4 Quoted from "The Swimmer: An Interview with Irving Layton," *op. cit.*

5 William Wordsworth, "Preface to Lyrical Ballads," in *William Wordsworth: Selected Poems and Prefaces*, ed. and intro. by Jack Stillinger (Boston: Houghton-Mifflin, 1965), p. 453.

6 William Henry Drummond, "The Voyager," from *Habitant Poems*, ed. Arthur Phelps (Toronto: McClelland and Stewart, 1970), p. 26.

7 Ernst Robert Curtius, *European Literature and the Latin Middle Ages*, tr. W.R. Trask (Princeton: Princeton University Press, 1973), p. 144. "The American Idiom" is William Carlos Williams' well-known phrase.

8 The words are Layton's, from *Taking Sides: The Collected Social and Political Writings*, ed. Howard Aster (Oakville: Mosaic Press, 1977), pp. 46-47.

9 Irving Layton, in "By Way of an Introduction: Poems for Twenty-Seven Cents" in *Engagements: The Prose of Irving Layton* (Toronto: McClelland and Stewart, 1972), p. 36.

10 Irving Layton, *Europe and other Bad News* (Toronto: McClelland and Stewart, 1979), p. 9.

11 Irving Layton, "Prince Hamlet and the Beatniks," in *Taking Sides, op. cit.*, p. 61.

12 George Bowering, "Irving Layton," in *West Window* (Toronto: General Publishing, 1982), p. 36.

13 Thomas Carlyle, "The Hero as Man of Letters," in *Selected Writings*, edited with an introduction by Alan Shelston (London: Penguin, 1971), p. 237.

14 Irving Layton, "There Were No Signs," in *A Wild Peculiar Joy* (Toronto: McClelland and Stewart, 1982), p. 94. All subsequent quotations from Layton's poems will be taken from this volume unless otherwise indicated.

15 In *The Collected Poems of Irving Layton* (Toronto: McClelland and Stewart, 1971), p. 484.

16 In *The Gucci Bag* (Oakville: Mosaic Press, 1983), p. 71.

17 The phrase "culture of crisis" comes from *Faces of Modernity: Avant-garde, Decadence, Kitsch* by Matei Calinescu (Bloomington: Indiana University Press, 1977), p. 265.

18 Walter Benjamin, *One-Way Street and Other Writings*, translated by Edmund Jephcott and Kingsley Shorter (Norfolk: NLB, 1979), pp. 157-159.

Leonard Cohen: The Endless Confessions of a Lady's Man

1 Leonard Cohen, "Go by Brooks," in *Selected Poems, 1956-1968* (Toronto: McClelland and Stewart, 1969), p. 49.

2 Quoted in "The Prophet as Celebrity," in *McGill Reporter*, January 20, 1969.

3 The phrase "folk lyrist" comes from Nietzsche's essay "The Birth of Tragedy," in *The Birth of Tragedy and The Case of Wagner*, tr. Walter Kaufmann (New York: Vintage, 1967), pp. 48-60. The entire discussion is of considerable relevance, especially the following quotation:

> First of all, however, we must conceive the folk song as the musical mirror of the world, as the original melody, now seeking for itself a parallel dream phenomenon and expressing it in poetry. *Melody is therefore primary and universal...* (p. 53)

It is also fascinating to recall that Nietzsche's essay gave Irving Layton the title of one of his best poems. As the Layton-Cohen friendship is well known, it would be interesting to speculate what influence Layton had on Cohen's early development.

4 "What I'm Doing Here," in *Selected Poems*, p. 87.
5 Leonard Cohen, *The Favourite Game* (London: Secker and Warburg, 1963), p. 101.
6 *Ibid.*, p. 25.
7 *Ibid.*, p. 102.
8 *Ibid.*
9 Quoted in *Leonard Cohen* by Stephen Scobie (Vancouver: Douglas and McIntyre, 1978).
10 Irving Howe, in "The Idea of the Modern," from *The Idea of the Modern in Literature and the Arts*, edited by Irving Howe (New York: Horizon Press, 1967), pp. 38-39.
11 "For My Biographers," Henry Moscovitch, *New Poems* (Oakville: Mosaic Press/Valley Editions, 1982), p. 12.
12 Leonard Cohen, "Stanzas for H.M." in *New Poems* by Henry Moscovitch, pp. 5-6.
13 Leonard Cohen, "How we loved you," in *The Energy of Slaves* (London: Jonathan Cape, 1972), pp. 115-116.

"Stone Angels":
An Essay on Margaret Laurence

1 Margaret Laurence, quoted in the Introduction to *Margaret Laurence*, edited by William New (Toronto: McGraw-Hill, 1977), p. 5.
2 Stendhal, *Scarlet and Black*, trans. by M.R.B. Shaw (London: Penguin, 1953), pp. 365-366.
3 Doris Lessing, Preface to *The Golden Notebooks* (St. Albans: Panther, 1973), p. 9.

4 John Fowles, *Daniel Martin* (Toronto: Collins, 1977), p. 3. For an interesting analysis of Fowles' novel, see John Gardner's *On Moral Fiction* (New York: Basic Books, 1977), pp. 50-52. I am indebted to Gardner's discussion for many things. Gardner's book has been unjustly neglected or scorned by American literary critics. He is, on occasion, off target, particularly in his flagrant misreading of Saul Bellow; but on the whole, his polemic on behalf of the moral dimensions of art is an antidote to "post-modern" posturings. Gardner does not include Laurence in his reading, but I am certain he would have understood her profoundly attentive and moral view.

5 *Ibid.*, p. 405.

6 "A Place to Stand On," from *Heart of a Stranger* (Toronto: Seal, 1976), p. 2.

7 Quoted in *Margaret Laurence, op. cit.*, p. 5.

"How to Act": An Essay on Margaret Atwood

1 R.D. Laing, "The Bird of Paradise," in *The Politics of Experience* (London: Penguin, 1967), p. 149.

2 *Ibid.*, p. 150.

3 Quoted in "Chatelaine Celebrity I.D.," *Chatelaine*, May, 1982, p. 44.

4 Quoted in *The Toronto Star*, May 18, 1982.

5 George Woodcock, "Margaret Atwood: Poet as Novelist," in *The World of Canadian Writing, Critiques and Recollections* (Vancouver: Douglas and McIntyre, 1980), p. 158.

6 Norman Mailer, *Existential Errands* (New York: Little, Brown, 1972), p. 187.

Odd Man Out

1 Robertson Davies, *Tempest-Tost* (Toronto: Clarke Irwin, 1951), pp. 11-12.

2 *Fifth Business* (Toronto: Macmillan, 1970), p. 2.
3 *The Manticore* (Toronto: Penguin, 1972), p. 53.
4 E.M. Forster, *Aspects of the Novel* (London: Penguin, 1974), p. 49.
5 "The Table Talk of Robertson Davies," in *The Enthusiasms of Robertson Davies*, ed. Judith Skelton Guest (Toronto: McClelland and Stewart, 1979), p. 311.
6 *Ibid.*, p. 314.
7 *Question-Time*, Preface (Toronto: Macmillan, 1975), p. xiii.
8 Then again, it may not: Saul Bellow's latest novels have that contemplative quality, too. This may be more a result of the author's vocation as a teacher. Read on in this essay.
9 *Ibid.*, p. viii.
10 *Ibid.*, p. ix.
11 For examples see *Studies in Robertson Davies' Deptford Trilogy*, edited by Robert G. Lawrence and Samuel L. Massey (Victoria: ELS, 1980), and Judith Skelton Guest's *Robertson Davies* (Toronto: McClelland and Stewart, 1978). An interesting rebuttal can be found in Anthony B. Dawson's essay "Davies, his Critics, and the Canadian Canon," *Canadian Literature*, No. 92, 1982, pp. 154-159.
12 Robertson Davies, "Jung and the Theatre," in *One Half of Robertson Davies* (Toronto: Macmillan, 1977), p. 145.
13 Quoted in Richard Ellmann's *James Joyce* (London: Oxford, 1959), pp. 689, 691-693.
14 Thomas Merton, "News of the Joyce Industry," in *The Literary Essays of Thomas Merton*, edited by Brother Patrick Hart (New York: New Directions, 1981), p. 15.
15 "Fifth Business" is explained in *Fifth Business, op. cit.*, pp. 266-267.
16 "Maple-Leaf Rabelais," review of *The Rebel Angels* by Anthony Burgess, *The Observer*, April 4, 1982, p. 93.